John M. Lundquist

The Temple

Meeting Place of Heaven and Earth

with 130 illustrations, 15 in color

Thames and Hudson

To my children

ART AND IMAGINATION

Any copy of this book issued by the publisher as a
paperback is sold subject to the condition that it
shall not by way of trade or otherwise be lent,
resold, hired out or otherwise circulated without the
publisher's prior consent in any form of binding or
cover other than that in which it is published and
without a similar condition including these words
being imposed on a subsequent purchaser.

© 1993 Thames and Hudson Ltd, London

First published in the United States of America in 1993 by
Thames and Hudson Inc., 500 Fifth Avenue,
New York, New York, 10110

Library of Congress Catalog Card Number 92-62138

Printed and bound in Singapore

Contents

Introduction

The temple incorporates within itself most of the ideas that make up our concept of religion. These include the idea of the centre, the sacred mountain, sacred waters and trees of life, sacred geometry, orientation to the four cardinal directions, initiation ritual, sacred dance, the mysteries, New Year festivals, ideas of cosmos/chaos and creation myths. It was within the setting of the temple that these other symbols, rituals and sacred textual traditions arose, and it is within the temple that they still have their deepest and truest meaning. Indeed, they can only be fully understood when they are reincorporated back into the context of the temple, and seen in that wider relationship.

Throughout all time, the temple has been the repository of the esoteric tradition. It was in the temple, and in the temple alone, that the knowledge of the mysteries could be found. These mysteries were recorded in books kept in the temple libraries, called 'Houses of Life' in ancient Egypt. But it was not a matter of 'book learning' alone, since the knowledge and understanding of the mysteries could only be transmitted through initiation ritual.

We can now begin to see how much more fundamental the temple is as the central ritual structure of the religious life than is commonly understood. If, in any religious culture, the temple dies out, as it did in Judaism for example after the destruction of the Temple of Jerusalem in 70 AD, at least two things happen: firstly, the scriptural and ritual tradition, which takes its meaning from the context of the temple, becomes, in the phrase of Jacob Neusner, a 'map without territory'. The ritual laws, the initiation rituals, become suspended in space, as it were, without a place in which they can be practised; and secondly, much of the ritual-initiation practice, previously carried out in an elaborate architectural setting, is transformed into a mental process; everything goes inward, is transferred onto the human body, and the mystical tradition is born.

This mystical tradition is, by definition, the transferral of the esoteric rituals and instructions from the sacred temple building into the mind of the practitioner. In Neusner's terms the 'territory' of the 'map' becomes the psychic processes of the individual. However, the body can also be at the ritual centre of temple initiation, as is the case in Indian temple Shiva ritual. The primordial creator god of Hinduism, Prajapati, became Purusa, the cosmic, universal person, whose sacrificed body was incorporated into the mandala floor plan of the Hindu temple.

The Temple's Many Names

'*Templum*', says the first-century BC Roman writer Varro, 'is the name given to a place set aside and limited by certain formulaic words for the purpose of augury or the taking of auspices.' From this come our words 'temple' and 'contemplate', which refer to the sacred, demarcated zone of the temple, that which was within the augur's range of vision, that which he 'contemplated'. Where there is no temple, there is, strictly speaking, no 'contemplation'.

The Latin root *tem* (to cut) has a cognate in Greek, *temno*, from which the word *temenos* derives. A *temenos* was 'a precinct, a piece of land marked off from common uses and dedicated to a god'. We now use *temenos* to mean the platform on which the temple building stands – an architectural structure that separated the building off from common, everyday activities. But the Greek root

Pre-Aztec model of a temple, from the Mezcala river region of Mexico.

has a much more ancient predecessor in Sumerian, *temen*, which meant a heaped-up pile of earth, as in the name of the Neo-Babylonian ziggurat (the traditional Tower of Babel), the *E-Temen-An-Ki*, the 'House of the Foundation of Heaven and Earth'.

Varro, in *De Lingua Latina*, states that there are three temples; of the sky, of the earth and of the underworld. We see this reflected in the Babylonian temple name and it brings us to the universal idea that there are three world regions in the cosmos: the sky, the earth and the underworld, all of which are united together in the temple, with its central pillar (sometimes, as in Scandinavia, a world tree), connecting the three zones.

We see this concept in ancient Sumer in one of the names given to a temple by King Gudea of Lagash, *temen abzu*, the Foundation of the Abyss. The *temen* in ancient Sumerian cosmology was seen as sunk down into the abyss. The temple pillars extended into the underworld regions, tying this region of the cosmos together with the earth and the sky.

The most common name for ancient Egyptian temples, *hwt ntr*, signified the manor or mansion of the god, the place where he lived, and where his ritual worship took place. Texts inscribed on the inner sanctum walls of the Ptolemaic period Temple of Edfu called that temple 'Foundation Ground of the Gods of the Beginnings', while the inner sanctum itself was called 'The High Seat', that is, the mythical mound of primordial creation.

The most widely known name for Hindu temples, Prasada, 'is made up of the presence of Shiva and Shakti, and of the Principles and Forms of Existence from the elementary substance Earth and ending with Shakti. The concrete form of Shiva is called House of God. So one should contemplate and worship it first.' The Prasada is brought into existence by the mantra *Nadi*, the primary vibration in the universe. In ancient Egypt, at Edfu, the temple was seen as coming into existence by the very process of the naming of its parts.

In Buddhism, one of the commonest names for the temple is 'Pagoda'. This word comes from the Sanskrit *dhatu-gharba* in which *dhatu* refers to the magical, sacred relics, particularly those related to the Buddha himself, which were kept in the temple, and *gharba* refers to the 'womb', the innermost sanctuary of the temple, in which Hindu temples was built deep within the centre of the temple, like a dark cave within a mountain. From *dhatu-gharba* comes the Sinhalese *dagoba*, which in Burma and other Southeast Asian countries becomes 'Pagoda'. The corresponding Sanskrit term is *stupa*, from Sanskrit *stup*, 'to accumulate or gather together'. Thus, deep within the temple, in its womb (in Buddhist pagodas or stupas the *harmika* or relic chamber is located above the domical base, which represents the *anda* or world egg), reside the sacred relics, with their *dhatus* (magic elements), which, like the egg, possess the power of life. The power of this womb and its world egg is transferred through the sacred altar that stands over the *gharba*, namely the *harmika*, and becomes a force for spiritual life and renewal.

The Mountain

In the beginning, there was water. Water has a two-fold imagery, life-giving and destructive. These two aspects, each represented by its avatar, fought one another at the beginning of the creative process, as described, for example, in the Babylonian creation account, *Enuma elish*. The battle was won by the forces of cosmos (in the case of *Enuma elish* this was Marduk), which defeated the chaotic waters and their serpent deity (in *Enuma elish*, Tiamat). With the end of this conflict, the waters subsided, and there appeared a mound of earth, the primary and primordial ground of creation, where the deity first appeared. This mound, charged with the energy of primordial life, became transformed into the sacred mountain, the most holy place on earth, the archetype of the temple. In virtually all cultures, temples are either the architectural representation of the primordial mound or of a world mountain or some combination of these two.

The Step Pyramid introduced by Egyptian king Zoser in the Third Dynasty was an architectural realization of the primordial hill, which was then modified into the true pyramid in the Fourth Dynasty. During the Ptolemaic Period, every temple was considered to be a replica of the primeval temple, which had been built upon the primordial mound after it had emerged from Nun, the primeval waters.

The canonical foundation ceremonies for temples in ancient Egypt included one ritual, 'hoeing the earth', that is directly related to the concept that the temple is the upward architectural extension out of the primeval waters of creation leading up into the sky above the primordial mound. In this ritual, the king would dig a pit with a hoe down to the water line. This founded the temple in the primordial waters.

The same conceptions are found in ancient Judaism, with the difference that in the place of the primeval mound a Foundation Stone appears. A famous passage in Midrash Tanhuma states:

> Just as the navel is found at the centre of a human being, so the land of Israel is found at the centre of the world. Jerusalem is at the centre of the land of Israel, and the temple is at the centre of Jerusalem, the Holy of Holies is at the centre of the temple, the Ark is at the centre of the Holy of Holies, and the Foundation Stone is in front of the Ark, which spot is the foundation of the world.

In ancient Israel, this Foundation Stone played the same role as the primordial mound in Egypt: it was the first solid material to emerge from the waters of creation, and it was upon this stone that the deity effected creation. According to Jewish legend, it was this primordial rock on which Jacob slept, at the place he subsequently named Bethel (Genesis 28). This same rock then came to be placed in the Holy of Holies of the Temple of Solomon, and, according to Islamic tradition, it is this same rock from which the Prophet Muhammed ascended into heaven, over which the second most sacred mosque of Islam, the Dome of the Rock, is built.

In ancient Sumer, the innermost sanctuary was sometimes referred to as the 'holy mound', and was seen as the mound which arose out of the primordial abyss. In this room the most sacred functions of Sumero-Babylonian religion were carried out. The temple itself grew up out of the abyss, in which it was founded, and became like a great mountain. The Holy of Holies of the main temple to the god Assur in ancient Assyria was called 'house of the great mountain of the lands'.

Perhaps no culture has so thoroughly created the architectural equivalent of a mountain in its temples as the Khmers of Cambodia, who, in the temples at Angkor, reproduced the mythical five peaks of the world mountain of the Hindu tradition, Mount Meru. And since Mount Meru, as the axis of the universe, was seen as reaching deep into the underworld, the bases of the Baphuon temple at Angkor were constructed in such a manner that they could not be seen. An inscription that relates to the Mebon Oriental pyramidal temple at Angkor states: 'In the middle of the sea, which is the sacred pool of Yasodhara, he erected a mountain, with a summit like that of Meru, covered with temples and sanctuaries plastered in stucco.'

Ancient Indian texts list as the first three types of temple Meru, Mandara and Kailasa, all of which are names given in the Indian tradition to the world mountain, which forms the axis of the universe.

The temple is a visual representation of all the symbolism of the mountain, and thus the architecture reflects this symbolism in a thoroughgoing and repetitive way (for example the pagoda structures of Indian, Chinese, Southeast Asian and Japanese temple architecture, with the multi-level hipped roofs present on every building and gateway in the complex, or the Prasada of the Hindu temple), and is a constant visual reminder that the visitor/initiate is engaged on a journey up a mountain, to heaven.

The mountain, a powerful earthly centre and point of contact with the heavens, became a gathering place for the celebration of seasonal rituals and for renewal ceremonies at the New Year. One of the main purposes of the New Year festivals was to rededicate the temple, to reestablish and reaffirm the peoples' connection with the gods in the heavens. Numerous temple reliefs, as well as reliefs on the walls of cities near the main gateways, depict the processions of kings and nobles, foreign peoples bearing fabulous gifts, all kinds of wheeled vehicles, and animals, approaching the city in order to attend the New Year festivals, where the rededication of the temple would signal the resumption of cosmic union and harmony.

The vegetation that the waters produced, which we can equate with the 'Tree of Life,' was luxurious, pristine and life-giving. This symbolism is exceptionally vivid in the Old Testament in reference to the messianic temple of the end of time, for example in Ezekiel: 'Then he brought me back to the door of the temple; and behold, water was issuing from below the threshold of the temple toward the east . . . (47:1) And on the banks, on both sides of the river, there will grow all kinds of trees for food' (47:12).

Other sources indicate that these waters flowed out from under the Holy of Holies, and were in fact held or capped in place by the Rock of Foundation or Foundation Stone, the Hebrew version of the primordial mound. A Neo-Sumerian temple hymn celebrates the temple with the line, 'Temple, at its top a mountain, at its bottom a spring.' Another ancient temple was referred to in an inscription as 'the House of the Plant of Life'. Temple architecture, paintings and reliefs depicted the 'primordial landscape', the world as it was in the beginning – mound, waters and trees of life (or other kinds of vegetation) in or near the Holy of Holies. An ancient Indian text states that 'The gods always play where groves are near, by rivers, mountains and springs, and in towns with pleasure gardens.' When King Jayavarman VII restored Angkor in the late twelfth century he had an inscription recorded at the four corners of the city which compared the wall of the city to the mountain chain that surrounds the universe, and the moat to the primeval ocean.

Within the mystical Islamic traditions the heavenly throne was said to rest on the primordial waters, which waters represented the entirety of the creation – spiritual and material. The heavenly throne descended to the earth, forming the

Kaabah in Mecca. Each of the four elements of the universe is represented in one of the four walls of the Kaabah (earth, air, fire, water), since the temple is the mirror image of the cosmos. Of these four, the northeast, or *Iraqi* corner represents the primordial waters, and it is at this corner that the well *zamzam* is located, out of which arise the living waters.

It is also at the northeast corner of the Kaabah that the Black Stone is to be found that embodies the essence and secret of the temple itself. According to Islamic Shiite tradition, the Black Stone originated as an angel who instructed Adam in the Garden of Eden. This angel had been the first in heaven to agree to covenant with God, and God had designated him as the one before whom all humankind would covenant each year. Upon Adam's expulsion from the Garden of Eden, this angel had taken the appearance of a White Pearl. Outside of the Garden, where Adam could no longer remember the promises he had made in the Garden, he noticed the White Pearl, but saw in it only a common stone. The Pearl then spoke to Adam, reminding him of the experiences in Eden. Adam then recognized his true self, kissed the Pearl, and renewed his covenant with God, promising that for ever after his posterity would likewise covenant themselves with God. The Pearl was then transformed into a Black Stone, symbolizing the darkness of this world, and it was this Stone that Adam, accompanied by the angel Gabriel, carried with him on his journey to Mecca. Upon his arrival in Mecca, the angels of heaven constructed a temple there that was the image of the temple where they had dwelt in heaven. Likewise, just as in heaven an angel had been the first to take an oath before God, so now that same angel, transformed into the Black Stone, was placed in the northeast corner of the Kaabah, so that the ritual of heaven could be performed yearly in the temple on earth. Thus at the northeast corner of the Kaabah pilgrims encounter both the Waters of Life, in the well *zamzam*, and the Black Stone, which symbolizes the recovery of the Paradisical situation of the Garden of Eden, and the establishment on earth of the heavenly model.

Just as was the case with the Stone of Foundation that was presumed to have been located within the Holy of Holies of the Temple of Solomon, so also the Black Stone of the Kaabah was the *umbilicus terrae*, the Navel of the Earth, the primary centre of the earth, and the place of initial creation. Indeed, in the early centuries after Christ's death, Christians generally believed that the Temple Mount had been superseded by Christ's burial place as the most holy place in Christendom, just as the New Testament had superseded the Old in Christian theology.

One of the most interesting ancient expressions of the association of temple and primeval waters is found in the account of the Temple of Atargatis in the north Syrian town of Hierapolis by the Syro-Greek writer Lucian. He reports that the inhabitants of the city believed that their temple had been founded over a 'chasm', which, following the end of the Great Flood, had opened up in the city and had swallowed up the flood waters. It was Deucalion, the Greek Noah, who had then built altars and a temple on the site of the chasm. In order to memorialize this event, the inhabitants of the entire area of north Syria would go twice yearly in formal processions to the sea where they would fetch water that would be returned to the temple and poured into the crevice inside the temple.

The Germanic and Scandinavian peoples also viewed mountains as particularly sacred. Place names that have been preserved in northern Europe, such as Wodansberge (the mountain of Wotan), and Odinsberg (in Scandinavia, the mountain of Odin), bear testimony to this. As was widely the case in antiquity, the coronation of the king, the decree of new laws or law codes, and other important royal acts were carried out in Scandinavia on the sacred mountain (or in its architectural counterpart, the temple). The Icelandic sacred place was the *Logberg*, located on a natural or man-made high place, where laws were decreed and where the king performed his royal functions.

According to Scandinavian mythology a gigantic world tree, Yggdrassil, united the three main world regions, with its roots sinking deep into the earth, while its branches reached into the heavens. A serpent lay at its roots; and an eagle nested in its heights. A number of sacred springs arose out of the depths of the earth at the tree's roots, including the spring of Mimir, the spring of wisdom and of life's mysteries. The springs at the roots of Yggdrassill restored one to health, as did the moisture that constantly dropped from its branches. The medieval historian Adam of Bremen, to whom we are indebted for a partial picture of the great Norse temple at Uppsala, in Sweden, reports that there was a huge evergreen flourishing at the temple. A spring emerged at its roots, to which sacrifices were made.

The Scandinavian World Tree is at the centre of the mythology of the Scandinavian shaman deity, Odin. A well-known phrase in the poem *Havamal* depicts Odin hanging on the tree, pierced with a spear: 'Nine nights I hung on the tree, wounded by a spear, dedicated to Odin, I myself to myself. I hung on a tree of which no one knows from which roots it grows . . . I sought below and lifted up the runic letters and I fell down from the tree.' The roots of the tree are in the underworld, the world of the dead, from which the spring Mimir, wisdom and divine knowledge, emerges. The shaman uses the World Tree as a vehicle to traverse the three cosmic zones, the heaven, the earth, and the underworld, since it encompasses all of these.

The cross on which Jesus was crucified carried similar symbolism, and it was indeed portrayed in early Christian iconography as a tree of life. The cross stood at the centre point of the world, Golgotha, the place where Adam, the first man, was buried. The blood of Christ dropped down onto the skull of Adam, revivifying him. The crucifixion of Jesus, as well as major episodes from Jesus' life, are interpreted in the New Testament within the context of temple symbols. The famous passage in Matthew 16:13–19 concerning the rock on which the church is built, against which the gates of hell will be impotent, can be related to Isaiah 28:16, :'I am laying a stone in Zion, a stone that has been tested, a precious cornerstone as a sure foundation.'; both refer to the Rock of Foundation in the Holy of Holies, which holds in place and caps the chaotic waters of the abyss. Jesus' reference in John 4:10 to the Samaritan woman about the 'living waters' that she will find by accepting him has meaning in the Old Testament concept of the 'living waters', or 'running waters', of Numbers 19:17, or the 'Fountain of Life' in Psalms 36:9.

Mayan temples were viewed as sacred mountains, the doors of which were seen as the entryways into the caves at the heart of the holy mountain. Deep within the cave the Tree of the World grew, denoting the *axis mundi*, the centre place of the cosmos. This tree grew up out of the Mayan underworld, Xibalba, and united all three of the main cosmic zones. A number of temples built together on a sacred platform thus represented a high mountain range, which towered over the tree stones on the floors of the plazas, representing a forest of trees. Sacred geography and sacred space then consisted of three elements: mountains, trees and caves.

The Heavenly Prototype

The inscriptions of the Sumerian king Gudea of Lagash place great emphasis on the temple as the *temen abzu*, the 'Foundation of the Abyss', or as the 'House of the Abyss', meaning that its foundations are sunk deep within the primordial waters, and rise up out of these waters. But there is another important aspect of the cosmology of the temple. Not only do creation and life come up out of the depths, *de Profundis*, they come down from the sky, from the heavens, the classic dwelling place of the gods. The basic idea is that there exists in the sky a perfect place, the 'city' of the gods. The goal of human life is both to establish contact with this place, and to return to it after death, thus to share in the life of the gods. The primary way by which the gods share with humans the knowledge of this place, and information on how one gets there, it through the temple. The earthly temple is an exact replica of a heavenly temple.

The god reveals to a king, prophet or shaman the architectural plan for the earthly temple, which is a replica of the heavenly temple. Exodus chapters 19 and 25 give us the classic pattern: the prophet ascends the mountain. There, the prophet is given a 'pattern' to examine. That 'pattern' is the temple (or here, tabernacle, the prototype of the Israelite temple in Jerusalem) which exists in heaven: 'According to all that I show you concerning the pattern of the tabernacle and of all its furniture, so shall you make it' (Exodus 25:9).

Likewise Ezekiel was 'brought . . . in the visions of God into the land of Israel, and [set] down upon a very high mountain, on which was a structure like a city opposite me' (Ezekiel 40:2). Here the prophet was taken in visions in order to measure the Temple of Solomon in Jerusalem. A heavenly messenger guiding him held 'a measuring reed in his hand' (Ezekiel 40:3). We find a similar motif in the Book of Revelation, where the Apostle John was visited by an angel and 'In the Spirit . . . carried . . . away to a great, high mountain' (Revelation 21:10). The angel 'had a measuring rod of gold to measure the city and its gates and walls' (Revelation 21:15). John had been transported to the mountain in order to view the Heavenly city of Jerusalem, which in the context of the Book of Revelation was one vast temple.

We see in both the Old and New Testament passages an important pattern, according to which the prophet is given a shaman-like vision on a mountain both prior to building the temple (where he views the heavenly model in order to transfer its architecture to the earth), and (as in the cases of Ezekiel and John), where he views either the temple or the heavenly temple-city prior to their *restoration* to the earth at the end of time.

The theme of the heavenly temple-city of Jerusalem, which at the end of time would be lowered down to earth, making of the entire earth one vast temple, persists throughout the Middle Ages, as can be seen in one of the illuminations to an early Spanish Beatus Apocalypse. There we see the plan view of the heavenly city, with John and the angel in the centre, the angel holding the golden measuring rod while John holds the book in which the revelations are recorded.

The earthly temple must incorporate features of the mountain. In India, a text states: 'Once heaven and earth were united. Let what is suitable to the sacrifice [namely, the temple] be common to both.' At Angkor the ancient Hindu cosmology of the central continent, Jambudpiva, encircled by six rings of mountain ranges, with seven oceans, and at the very centre, the world mountain Meru, was exactly reproduced during the ninth to twelfth centuries AD. The world of the gods was brought down to the world of humans, bringing the two into the contact that assured that prosperity and life would flow from the gods to humans, through the presence and ritual of the temples.

The Kaabah in Mecca, Islam's holiest shrine, is seen as the exact image of the heavenly throne or temple, and is thus the centre of the terrestrial world. The architecture of the heavenly model descended onto the earth, taking the form of the straight sides of the earthly temple (the cube-shaped Kaabah), symbolizing the possibility of direct communication between heaven and earth.

Of all temple building cultures of the world, the peoples of the Valley of Mexico were most profoundly influenced in their temple ritual and architecture by cosmic concepts. The pyramid-temple complexes of Mayan cities reproduced on earth the sacred landscape created by the gods at the beginning of time. The Pyramid of the Sun, the central pyramid in the Avenue of the Dead complex at Teotihuacan (known anciently as 'the place where man becomes divine'), dates to the Classic Period – 150 BC–750 AD. It was constructed according to an extensive astronomical symbolism. The pyramid was built over a previous shrine, which in turn was built over a subterranean cave which had long been the centre for cult practices. The cave itself was a seven-pronged chamber which figures in the Maya creation account, the *Popul Vuh*, as the place where the ancestors first emerged (the Aztecs later buried their rulers in this cave). The earthly city was seen as the exact mirror image of the heavenly city, with the major axis – the Avenue of the Dead – and the temples and pyramids built along that axis oriented astronomically to the Pleiades, the four cardinal directions, and the surrounding mountains. The numerous platforms situated along the Avenue of the Dead are actually connected more with the universe through the cosmic orientation than with each other as parts of a more traditional architectural arrangement. The cave directly underneath the Pyramid of the Sun was illuminated by the sun each year at the Summer solstice. Here we see the two main concepts that have been emphasized above: the sacred place rising up out of the underworld, the place from which life comes, and its architectural plan brought down out of the heavens.

In ancient Egypt and Mesopotamia, in the Bible, and in Mesoamerica, the king is pre-eminently a builder, a builder of temples. The plan of the temple can only come to him through contact with the sacred, either through direct revelation, or through fundamental grounding, plus initiation, in the sacred texts and traditions. The famous statue of King Gudea of Lagash shows him holding on his lap the lapis lazuli plan of the temple that had been revealed to him in a dream during his night in a temple.

Thus, in the ancient temple-building societies, order did not exist, the earth was not cosmicized, society did not function properly, the law codes could not be decreed, except in a temple established on earth that was the authentic and divinely revealed counterpart of a heavenly prototype.

Sacred Geometry

By sacred geometry we mean a mathematics which had as its purpose the accurate laying out of the temple ground plan in relation to the cardinal directions and to the heavens; in other words, the ritually proper and absolutely accurate transferral of the heavenly plan onto the earth. The temple is the reduced plan of the cosmos, and as such must be an accurate representation of the heavenly prototype. Accuracy is vitally important. A wrong orientation would bring death, destruction and all manner of disasters.

All of these considerations made the actual preparation of the site and laying of the foundations actions that were immersed in ritual. Chief among these was the 'stretching of the cord', well attested in both ancient Egypt and India, a kind of 'sacred surveying', which established the ground plan of the building, set its four corners – oriented to the cardinal directions – and brought the earthly building into relationship with the gods of the heavens and the constellations, or the gods in their guise as constellations.

The ritual of stretching the cord is known in Egypt from as early as the Second Dynasty king Khasekhemwy to as late as the Ptolemaic Period Temple of Edfu (built between 237 and 57 BC). The astronomical ceiling from the unfinished tomb of Senmut at Deir el-Bahri (about 1458 BC) gives a fascinatingly clear view of the astronomical underpinnings of this rite. The rite continued virtually unchanged over several thousand years, and in fact the Edfu texts state that the ritual of stretching the cord originated with the legendary architect, sage, physician and magician, Imhotep of the reign of Djoser (Third Dynasty).

In the Egyptian ritual, which took place during the night, at the time of the new moon, the sky was first 'stretched out', its ultimate boundaries determined and set out with particular reference to the constellation known in Egyptian as *Mshtjw*. The goddess Seshat, 'Mistress of the ground plans and the writings', 'Lady of plans, Lady of writings in the House of Life', working together with the king, acting as the son of god, as Horus, and also with Thoth, god of the ground plans and the construction prescriptions, led in the surveying procedures.

On a night of the new moon, when *Mshtjw* (Ursa Major) could be observed, the heavens were laid out. At the same time, still during the night, the surveying cord was stretched out over the temple site, establishing the four corners of the building. In the tomb of Senmut, two transit lines extend across the northern part of the ceiling, and attach themselves to the lower portion of *Mshtjw*. These lines have been interpreted as a visual representation of the process of sighting on the circumpolar stars, and have been associated with a well known 'Stretching of the Cord' text, which states, in part, 'I have grasped the peg . . . I observe the forward-striding movement of the constellations. My eye is fixed on the Great Bear. I . . . determine the corners of your temple' (quoted in S. Giedion, *The Beginnings of Architecture*).

This text is found at the Edfu Temple, and forms a part of the construction texts found in the main shrine and on the exterior of the enclosure wall. With the passing of the night and the rising of the sun god, Re, the chaos of the dark but starry night is overcome, and cosmos is established, cosmos that consists of the coordination of the heavens with the earth, centred in the earthly temple.

In another Egyptian example of this ritual, the texts accompanying the relief scenes in the temple of Seti I, at Abydos (about 1305–1290 BC), show the king and Sefkhet-'Abwy (as Seshat was known at that period), laying out the temple foundation lines before Osiris. The text has Sefhet-'Abwy saying: 'It is Ptah who lays out its foundations in person; it is thy father Re who establishes it like his horizon.' Osiris then says: 'I cause thy mansion to abide like the sky.' The scene is titled 'Stretching the cord in the Mansion of Usimare-setepenre [the Prenomen of Ramesses II, the son of Seti I, and the finisher of this temple], near to the necropolis.'

Tibetan mandalas are drawn out on the ground according to the most minutely detailed ritual instructions. The initial lines are laid down with a white cord. For the subsequent lines, five threads (sutra) of the finest quality, each of a different colour and twisted together, are dipped in coloured powder. The cord (called 'the cord of gnosis') is then stretched out along the ground, demarcating the line of the mandala. When the cord has been stretched taut, it is raised up and allowed to fall suddenly, leaving a residue of coloured powder to form the proper line on the ground. This procedure is repeated numerous times, until the general outlines of the mandala are achieved. All aspects of the cord stretching ceremonies are described in the Tibetan treatises in extreme detail, including the lengths of the cord, purification rituals, and so on. The five cords represent the five Buddha families (detailed below in connection with Borobudur). The central axis of the mandala, representing the axis mundi, Mount Meru, is drawn by a cord called 'Thread of Brahma', which is used to establish the median north to south and east to west lines.

In India, the temple was always built only after observing the stars for favourable configurations. The images of the regents of the planets and the stars were carved into the walls of the temple. Indeed, the very plan of the Indian temple, the Vastupurusamandala, had represented on it the 32 Naksatras, the constellations that the moon passes through on its monthly course. The astrologer consulted these at every stage in the temple building: the determination of the purification of the soil, the insemination of the ground, the levelling of the site, the determination of the cosmic orientation of the building, the construction and placing of the altar, and the stretching of the cord as the mandala was laid out on the ground; in each case determinations were made according to the place of the sun, the moon, or one of the planets within the circle of the heavenly bodies that were represented on the sacred ground plan.

In Egypt, temple sites were given magical protection through a rite of circumambulation by the gods, in which statues or images for all gods for whom the temple was being built were carried around the site, clockwise. Circumambulation is a ritual act that commemorates the journey of the sun god through the heavens, and thus further cosmicizes the building.

Perhaps no temple complex has ever been so thoroughly and minutely oriented to the heavenly bodies as Angkor Wat, built by Suryavarman II over a thirty-year period during the early twelfth century AD. Recent exhaustive astronomical studies conducted at the site and published in Science have shown that the temple entrances, which, in contrast to other temples in Cambodia, were constructed facing west, ensured that the rising sun was directly aligned across the topmost tower precisely at the entrance on the equinox and solstice days (which correlates with the worship of the sun god Vishnu by the builder, King Suryavarman II, who died in 1150). Altogether, twenty-two positions within the temple were used to observe the sun and the moon. Most astonishing of all, the east–west axis of the temple recorded, in architectural distances, both the passing of the 365-day year, and the four major periods of Hindu cosmology: the Krita, Treta, Dvapara and Kali Yugas. Furthermore, the two worst and most degenerate Yugas, Kali and Dvapara, were arranged along the axis so that they were the farthest in distance from the main shrine of the temple, which is nestled inside the base of the central tower, which represents the central peak of Mount Meru, the centre and axis of the universe.

Various traditions within Islam give two complementary accounts of the building of the Kaabah in Mecca. In the first of these, a tent from among the tents in Paradise is lowered onto the earth, fitting exactly the space into which the Kaabah was constructed. In various traditions the tent is put into place by the Angel Gabriel, other angels, or by God himself. The tent is fastened with four pegs of gold, symbolizing universal nature in its four-fold division. The ropes of the tent were of silken thread as fine as hair, and were violet in colour, representing the emanations of the Light of the Soul. The tent's central pillar was of red hyacinth. Red was taken to be a combination of white (the dimension of Light) and black (the dimension of Darkness), thus symbolizing the Divine, which intermingles the duality of light and darkness.

According to the second tradition, Adam was taken to the site of the Kaabah by the Angel Gabriel, carrying with him the Black Stone. Upon their arrival at the site, a white cloud descended from heaven and enveloped them. Gabriel commanded Adam to trace with his foot a groove in the earth that corresponded exactly to the shadow cast by the cloud. This became the exact outline of the Kaabah. Gabriel then instructed Adam to continue tracing the outline of the heavenly cloud, and this became the precincts of the sacred *haram*, the area that surrounds the Kaabah. The Black Stone was then desposited in the northeast corner, as a symbol of the heavenly compact made between God and his creatures, and it was on this spot that the sons of Adam brought their sacrifice to God.

The role of sacred geometry in Mayan temples of the Peten region in Guatemala has been extensively documented. Many such temples were constructed for geomantic purposes, with elaborate sight lines on the sun, moon or stars. Of particular importance are the three Group E temples at Uaxactun, north of Tikal. Here, three small temples stood on a north-south axis across a courtyard from a pyramid facing east. These temples marked the solstice and equinox cycles of the sun. From the pyramid steps the sun arose directly over the central temple on the equinoxes, over the southernmost on the winter solstice and the northernmost at the summer solstice. Such arrangements were meant to reflect the cosmic order in the arrangement of the courtyards, with their temples and platforms, the entire ensemble connected with the heavens by means of astronomical sight lines.

At Tikal, also in the Peten region (Classic Period, 300–900 AD), the Temple of the Giant Jaguar (Temple I), on the eastern side of the Great Plaza, was built in nine architectural levels, expressing the Mayan view of the nine underworld regions. Mayan ideas of solar cycles and other calendric information were incorporated into the architecture of the building. In the same complex at Tikal there are ceremonial complexes consisting of twin platforms with stairs on four sides, facing each other at the east and west ends of a temenos. Since there are no temples on top of the platforms, they may have served for ritual performances or sacred dance within the temple complex. There are nine monolithic stele in front of the west platform, with a round altar in front of each stela. A long building on the northern edge of the temenos has nine doors. These 'twin complexes' were built to commemorate a *katun*, a sacred calendric cycle of twenty years.

Among the Germanic peoples a sacred pole, the Irminsul, was thought to hold up the heavens and was considered to be the cosmic world pillar. Charlemagne destroyed the Irminsul and sacred woods of the temple in Erisburg in 772 AD. According to Rudolph of Fulda (*c.* 860), this column was the 'column of the universe holding up almost all things'. Sometimes such pillars would be tilted towards the north, thus representing the axis of the universe. The pillar on the earth was a model of the pillar in heaven, thus the heavenly spheres revolved around the earthly temple. Nails would be driven into the pillar, representing the Pole Star, and it was along this pillar that the shaman ascended into heaven. With this central pillar in place, uniting the world regions (the pillar also extends to the underworld) the prophet or king or shaman could also enter the temple at night in order to have numinous dreams. Thus Gudea of Lagash entered the temple, where he received a message through a dream that he was to build a temple to the god Ningirsu.

The combination of the central pillar and the dream come together in the dream that Jacob had at Bethel (Genesis 28). He slept on the primordial stone, the place where creation on earth was carried out by God. During his sleep Jacob dreamt of a ladder 'set up on the earth, and the top of it reached to heaven; and behold, the angels of God were ascending and descending on it' (Genesis 28:12). God then gave him the message that 'the land on which you lie I will give to you and to your descendants' (13). The ladder is the prototype of the pillar which unites heaven and earth. Upon awakening Jacob was overcome with the awesomeness of the place, and exclaimed: 'This is none other than the house of God, and this is the gate of Heaven' (17). He then designated the place as *Beth El*, Bethel, the House of God (i.e., the temple) (22).

It was the custom among the ancient Sumerians and their predecessors in Iraq to incorporate the foundations of crumbling temples into new structures, thus incorporating the sanctity and numinous power of the previous temple. The old building would be filled in with mud bricks, then levelled off, providing a building platform on which the new temple would rise. This process is documented in the temple precinct at the site of Eridu, the first Sumerian city, and at Uruk and other cities, for over one thousand years during the Ubaid and Uruk Periods. The great majority of Classical Greek temples were founded on the remains of earlier Mycenaean temples. The Temple Mount of Jerusalem, where the Dome of the Rock stands today, has a tradition as a sacred temenos going back at least four thousand years. According to the Old Testament accounts, the place where Abraham (about 2000 BC) was commanded to sacrifice Isaac was the sacred high place, Mount Moriah. This same place was the threshing floor that David (about 1000 BC) bought from Araunah the Jebusite, 'in order to build an altar to the Lord' (2 Samuel 24:21). The threshing floor in the ancient world carried the symbolism of the omphalos, or the navel of the world, thus an emblem of the universe (a round piece of earth, with the axis in the middle, with the oxen of the sun going around it). This then became the place where Solomon erected the Temple of the Lord (after about 960 BC), 'His holy mountain, beautiful in elevation' (Psalms 48:2).

The Mandala

The primary expression of sacred geometry in temple architecture is the mandala. The mandala is a sacred, numinous shape consisting of the intersection of a circle (the shape of the heavens) and a square (the primary shape on the earth's surface). Mandalas have been called 'graphic mirrors of supernatural essences', and 'maps of the cosmos'. By their very nature they cosmicize a building constructed to be a temple, and establish that building as the centre, with the world tree at its axis, uniting the three main levels of the universe and sanctifying the four world regions.

But it goes beyond the architectural, and particularly in Tantric Buddhism, is transferred or projected onto the human body, where all the features of the painted or architectural mandala are represented at the appropriate places in the body, the Chakras. Furthermore, in Tantrism, the mandala is the focal point of meditation techniques. No actual or visible mandala need be present as the initiate experiences the journey to enlightenment in the mind, all the architectural details of the mandala are present in the visualization process. This is expressed in one text in the following manner: 'The body becomes a [mandala] palace, the hallowed basis of all the Buddhas.' In this sense, the mandala becomes what has been called a psychocosmogram. A sand or coloured powder mandala can sanctify the place, however secular may be its basic purpose and use, as, for example, in the Paramount Theater in Madison Square Garden in New York City, during October 1991. Rituals were carried out that prepared the auditorium for initiation ceremonies, and as a result it became 'the sacred mandala palace of Kalachakra', with the initiate visualizing himself seated at the eastern door.

The basic ground plan of the Hindu temple is founded on a mandala that bears the name *Vastupurusamandala*. The component parts of this Sanskrit word, and their meanings, are: *vastu*, 'that which exists in an ordered state'; *purusa*, 'universal, supernal, or cosmic man (the unconditioned self)'; and *mandala*, 'the numinous shape'. The *Vastupurusamandala* is square, because in India the square is the paramount, perfect shape, signifying order, finality and perfection. The circle emanates from the square, is thus derivative from it, and signifies growth and movement. The circle symbolizes our present world, the square the perfect world of the heavens. The round earth and the square heaven are joined by the four cardinal directions, primarily east and west, the places of the rising and setting sun, where the earth and heaven come closest together. Thus, the earth and sky themselves, in their union, form a mandala.

The most extraordinary architectural expression of a mandala is the temple of Borobudur, in the centre of Java. Borobudur, perhaps the most magnificent example of sacred architecture in the world, was built during the eighth and ninth centuries by the Buddhist Sailendra dynasty. Borobudur encompasses everything that we can posit of temple architecture, symbol and ritual. It is at once a mountain, and a magnificent mandala of the Tantric (esoteric) type well known in Tibet and Nepal.

Borobudur stands in the Kedu Plain in central Java, south of a line of 10,000–12,000 foot high volcanoes. Its intimate relationship to the volcanoes can be seen in the etymology of the name of the ruling family that built the monument – Sailendra, 'Lords of the Mountain'. It appears to have been constructed away from any major city, and fits beautifully the pattern of a pilgrimage mountain-temple (in a natural paradise). There is evidence that Chinese pilgrims continued to visit the site even after it had been abandoned locally and Javanese civilization had shifted further to the east of the island. Its famous plan, widely illustrated, is probably the best known mandala configuration in the world.

Borobudur is a structure with a square base, oriented towards the four cardinal directions, and with four monumental staircases in the middle of each face. Six lower levels are square, with returns and projections, while there are four upper, circular terraces, the topmost of which supports the central stupa. Each staircase goes all the way to the topmost terrace. Of the six lower terraces, the middle four consist of galleries with relief sculptures, which completely enclose the pilgrim on both sides, but are open to the sky. The base of the lowest level was decorated with reliefs showing the underworld 'hell worlds', but these are no longer visible, except for one section in the so-called 'hidden foot'.

The galleries were meant to be circumambulated in a clockwise direction (*pradakshina*), so that the initiate could observe and 'read' the reliefs, which gradually took him to ever greater spiritual heights as he gradually circumambulated and ascended to the higher levels. Within each gallery, the outer balustrade wall contains two levels of reliefs, while the inner or gallery wall contains one level. The entire series is a continuous narrative, consisting of tales and stories from the previous lives of the Buddha, his earthly life, and stories of previous Buddhas. From the second to the fourth galleries the reliefs recount the spiritual wanderings of the pilgrim Sudhana, who sought out numerous teachers in his quest to become a bodhisattva, and who finally, as depicted at the end of the series of reliefs in the fourth gallery, gained entrance into the palace of the Buddha-to-be, Maitreya, on Mount Sumeru.

The first three upper, circular terraces contain 72 stupas, 32 on the first circular level, 24 on the second, and 16 on the third. The *anda*, or domical section of each stupa, was constructed with stone lattice work, so that one can see the inside of the dome. The stupas on the two lower circular levels have diamond-shaped lattice work, with square *harmikas* (the altar on top of the dome), while those on the third level show square lattice work and octagonal *harmikas*. Each of the stupas contained a seated Buddha figure, his hands forming a mudra which has been variously identified as *dharmachakra* (turning of the wheel of law) or *bodyhyangi-mudra* (member of enlightenment). Each Buddha could be seen through the lattice work. The topmost stupa originally contained a Buddha figure, (later stolen), which some scholars believe was of the Adibuddha, hidden within the dome of the structure and thus out of view to pilgrims. The Adibuddha is the primordial Buddha, the primal, non-dual essence, the source of universal mind, from which everything emanates, that is, from which the physical universe originates. Adibuddha is unborn and uncreated, exists spontaneously, without cause or dependent origination, and yet is the ultimate cause and originator of everything in the universe.

On the lower, gallery levels, five balustrades are formed that look out over the plain in each direction. Seated within niches ranged along each balustrade, facing the four directions, are, in total, 432 Buddhas. The Buddhas on each side of the temple on the first four balustrades all sit in the same posture, with the same mudra. Those on the east sit in *bhumispharsa*, 'touching the earth', and represent the *Dhyani* or meditation Buddha Akhshobya; those on the south make the gesture of *varada*, 'greeting', corresponding to the Dhyani Buddha Ratnasambhava; the Buddhas on the west side sit with the mudra of *dhyani*, 'meditation', and represent Amitabha; while those on the north face of the monument express the gesture of *abhayamudra*, 'fearlessness', the mudra of the Dhyani Buddha Amoghasiddhi. The Buddhas in the niches of the fifth balustrade level, 64 in all, all form the same mudra in each direction, *vitarkamudra*, 'teaching', and represent the Dhyani Buddha Vairocana. The total number of Buddhas in the niches along the balustrades is 432, one of the most important numinous numbers within the Indian religious tradition, symbolizing a *mahayuga*, 4,320,000, the total time of the four world ages; Kritayuga, Tretayuga, Dvaparayuga and Kaliyuga.

The Buddhas in the niches of the four faces have the appearance, from a distance, of Siddhas, or hermits, meditating deep within caves on the sides of the sacred mountain. The circumambulating initiate would rise ever higher up the holy mountain, learning the sacred doctrines through the reliefs, ascending through the world as we know it, to the level of inner vision, of meditation, leaving the world of appearances, and reaching, as it were, the foothills of Mount Meru, in the Himalayan range. This is not the highest, formless, state of existence, because he can still see (though with some difficulty through the lattice work) the meditating Buddhas inside the stupas. Finally, he would reach the level of the topmost stupa, the summit of the cosmic mountain, Mount Meru, within which the essence of all existence, the Adibuddha, symbolizing formlessness and emptiness, sat, but out of view to the human eye. This would have been at the exact centre of the topmost, domical stupa, at the axis of the world mountain, and thus of the universe.

Borobudur has been placed within the context of the Tibetan and Nepalese Tantric traditions of Diamond World Mandalas, which have their architectural expression in the Himalayan regions in the so-called Adibuddha Stupas, the most famous example of which is the Kum-Bum Temple at Gyantse, in Tibet. Kum-Bum, built about five hundred years later than Borobudur, has virtually the same top plan as Borobudur, although its upper, circular terraces are, in typical Tibetan style, domical, not open. In this conception the Adibuddha, the formless, non-dual centre and source of all emanation, is seen at work at each level of the temple-mountain: the hell worlds, the form realms of earthly existence, and in his manifestations as the five Dhyani Buddhas, who represent the five-fold transcendent wisdom of the Adibuddha.

The five Dhyani Buddhas have each presided over a world system. The pilgrim or initiate comes to the temple to learn the essence of a vast cosmic world-system (thus for example the role of the measurement of the Kalpas in temples such as Angkor Wat and Borobudur), and thus ultimately about creation itself. One learns also the insubstantiality of all appearance.

The mandala as an expression of sacred geometry is deeply rooted in the architecture of early Christian churches. This can be seen most vividly in the vault directly over the main altar at San Vitale in Ravenna (dedicated in 547 AD). Much of the symbolism of the temple comes together in this magnificent mosaic. Jesus represented as the Lamb of God stands at the centre of the mandala configuration, which represents the starry night sky as well as the celestial Church. Four angels hold up the vault of heaven, with the Lamb in the centre, surrounded by stars, representing resurrection. The heavenly tabernacle is filled with plants and animals that are reminiscent of the pristine paradise, the place of first creation, that is so often represented in the architecture or painted illustration of the temple.

Ritual

To benefit from the temple ordinary mortals must approach it with great care. The temple is a dynamo, a place of considerable power. The numinous is both life-giving and dangerous. Ordinary mortals, indeed priests too, approach the temple through ancient, carefully prescribed ritual preparations, including purification, special clothing, certain ritual movements and gestures (*mudra*), ritual speech (*mantra*), visual symbols (*yantra*) and group interaction. These rituals are not something recently thought up or devised in popular religious or artistic movements (although traditional forms of ritual may well appear in these media). They bear the stamp of tradition, are often passed on by elderly members of a society, are usually considered to be secret, and are purposefully kept from the knowledge of outsiders, or those who have not been initiated.

Ritual is the primary means that makes communication possible between humans and the powers beyond immediate human life – the transcendent. Ritual is the process through which contact with the world of the numinous powers is activated. It is not something dry, ossified, or meaningless, as it is widely thought to be in the Western world (cf. the word 'ritualistic'). It is a means of access to spiritual power.

One simply does not and cannot approach the transcendent powers casually. And one cannot make up one's own agenda in communicating with such powers. One must look to the past, to the written tradition, and to the authorized masters who have received such knowledge through oral tradition. These traditions can only be kept alive by ongoing communication between humans and the transcendent, through a living ritual tradition – in the temple.

The means of approach and of arrival are what we understand in the term 'ritual'. Even where we speak of 'the temple built without hands', in other words the 'psychocosmogram' such as the interior mandala, or the interior Kabbalistic tradition, a master teacher – a guru – is needed to guide the initiate.

Within the Tibetan tradition of Secret Mantra Vajrayana three assumptions are made about initiation: 1) the hall or room where the initiation is taking place is the Pure Realm; 2) the Lama directing the initiation is the Primordial Buddha; 3) the initiates are receiving secret oral teachings. The etymology of the Tibetan word for 'initiation' is 'conferral of power'. At the beginning of each teaching or initiation within Tibetan Buddhism the Lama conducting the ceremony recites to the initiates his own 'chain of authority', going into great detail, and tracing the authority back to the Buddha himself. It is such authority that makes possible, as I mentioned above, the transformation of the Paramount Theatre in New York City into the 'Mandala Palace of Kalachakra'.

Thus, ritual is not a casual new invention. It is as old as the temple itself, and must be carefully followed, lest harm result. I am not talking here about forms of customary or oft-repeated human behaviour, such as walking my dog in the same direction each morning and buying the morning paper at exactly the same time – actions that many speak of as 'ritual.' I am referring to religious liturgies in which every detail of the performance is specified, and opportunities for variation are narrowly limited.

Knowledge of this ritual is the secret, esoteric tradition that is kept in the temple libraries as books, manuscripts or in some other written form, and that is passed on orally, as a secret doctrine by acknowledged teachers and masters.

But if information on the secret tradition is contained in books, can one not learn about this tradition simply by reading such books, many of which are widely published and accessible today? The answer is no. This is evident if one compares, say, the *Kalachakra Tantra Rite of Initiation*, recently edited and translated by Jeffrey Hopkins, with the actual initiation ceremony. There is much that occurs during the ceremony that would not be understood by one who had only read the book. The initiation must be *experienced* under the guidance of an authorized master, who administers oaths and gives instructions, many of which belong to the secret, oral tradition, and are accompanied by information not otherwise available to the uninitiated.

The emphasis on authority figures and on the great age of rituals does not mean that innovations do not occur. But when they do occur, the change takes place within the context of the authority structure, and the changes would not be so drastic that the resultant rituals would be unrecognizable to adherents. Within modern, technological society we value change, and are used to yearly change in many customs and technologies. But in the great religious traditions, change is viewed with suspicion, especially if it is imposed from outside the traditional authority structures.

Some ritual is related to the shape of the sacred mountain, or to the sphericity of the heavens, or the course of the sun. These three could provide a partial explanation for one of the most basic ritual movements, circumambulation, which is present in most of the ritual of world religion. Circumambulation represents totality, perfection and taking (inner, spiritual) possession.

Another common type of ritual movement is to walk upward, which can be related to the journey up the sacred mountain. A third is to walk inward, to the interior of the sanctuary, where the most holy place is to be found. These three important types of ritual movement can all be seen in the ritual journey of the initiate at Borobudur: circumambulating the galleries, ascending in height at each new gallery, moving ever inward toward the centre of the mountain-temple. Thus one walks around, upward and inward, to the centre. In Egyptian temples, each successive threshold rose to a higher level, until one reached the highest elevation in the back of the temple, in the inner sanctum, representing the primordial mound of creation.

Other forms that ritual movement may take include dance, speech and vigorous body movement, all of which, with some exceptions, take place within a group setting, since temple ritual is one of the most powerful social bonding mechanisms in traditional societies. Ritual is related to the establishment of a harmonious society through group interaction and celebration of stages in the human and natural life cycle, and observation of the calendric cycle of festivals. The kinds of movement, and of preparation, such as purification, changing of

This section through the temple of Dendera, Egypt, clearly illustrates the worshipper's progress from the outside world through increasing degrees of sacredness to the holy of holies. The entrance is on the left, the innermost sanctuary on the right.

clothes, and so forth, that come to be required in order to approach a temple, are canonized, and, once canonized, persist through many generations and become very widespread geographically.

Greek drama has been thought to have originated in the initiation rites dedicated to Dionysus. The central feature of the Dionysiac and Orphic rites at such shrines as Delphi, Eleusis and Agrae was the worshipper's belief that he could actually become one with and share the destiny of Dionysus or Orpheus, just as in Egypt initiates shared the destiny of Osiris, and in Christianity the destiny of Christ. There was a strong pantomimic element in the Dionysiac cults, in which initiates played the roles of various deities in the cycle of dramatic stories revolving around that deity. The end result of the rituals was that the initiate would overcome the effects of death. Plutarch consoled his wife upon the death of their young daughter by telling her that she should remember 'the mystic symbols of the rites of initiation to Dionysus'.

The Omphalos or Navel of the World, the primordial tumulus stone, symbol of the Earth Mother and of Dionysus, was also a centre piece of the rituals at Delphi, Agrae and Eleusis. Here the initiate came, dancing the ecstatic ritual dance before the Omphalos, on which Greek vase paintings depict Dionysus seated. Initiation thus centred on the supreme oracle, the seat of life and of revelation of the mysteries of death and of the world beyond.

Within Islam, the primary ritual action of the Pilgrimage – circumambulation seven times around the Kaabah – originates in Heaven. Just as in Heaven the angels walk around the Divine Throne, so on earth human beings walk around the earthly model of the Heavenly Throne. Just as the earthly temple is based on a heavenly archetype, so also is earthly ritual based on heavenly ritual. The number seven is archetypal, representing the seven millennia of earthly existence, as well as the seventy thousand angels who surround the Heavenly Throne, the seven divine attributes, and the seven veils that separate God from humankind. Ritual thus also partakes of sacred geometry. What exactly does circumambulation represent in esoteric Islam, other than being a pattern of heavenly action? It is a process of taking possession of totality, of encircling, encompassing, as well as being encompassed by, universal intelligence. It signifies the restoration within oneself of the White Pearl, restored from the Black Stone, restoring within oneself the celestial body of light which originates in the heavenly realms and is to be found in the earthly model of the celestial, the Kaabah.

Erich Neumann called ritual 'the archetype of the way'. The earliest 'way' into the centre that is recorded in human experience, he believed, is to be found in the Upper Paleolithic caves of Europe. Fundamental to the cave shrines of Laussel, Pech Merle, and Lascaux was the dark, dangerous journey into the deep interior of the caves, where the shrines were created and the wall paintings executed. From these early experiences, Neumann proposed, came concepts of ritual that are still with us today. Underlying all temple ritual is the idea of the mysteries that are preserved there, and of the difficult, labyrinthine journey of initiation that one must take to reach the centre. Furthermore, one needs a leader, a teacher, one who has already experienced the danger of the way since he has himself been initiated. The prototypes of these concepts Neumann found in the Upper Paleolithic caves, with the dark, dangerous journey one would have had to take to reach the interior, and the mysteries of the Great Mother that originated there.

Ritual Drama in the Temple

The mysteries of the temple take many forms, differing from culture to culture, and are in fact in many ways culture specific, as we would expect. Two types of temple initiation, however, are particularly widespread, and these are the 'theatrical' staging of ritual performances based on the creation myths, and the initiation of the living into the knowledge and mysteries of the afterlife.

Already in 1867 the great pioneer of Egyptology, Lepsius, wrote: 'The Book of the Dead, or the collection of the texts relating to the resurrection, the judgment, and the life in the other world, was in its essential character a book of practical instruction. Its aim was to inform the individual, intent on his spiritual welfare, about what already on earth should be *known* and *prepared* by him for his death'.

Thus, creation and death were the two grand themes, and it was these that informed the ritual processes of the temples and benefitted the relative few who could actually gain access to them. The best-known example from ancient Egypt of a ritual drama based on a creation text is the so-called 'Theology of Memphis', the famous Shabaka Stone. Pharaoh Shabaka (712–698 BC) of the Twenty-fifth Dynasty discovered an ancient text in a temple in Memphis, a text relating the creation according to the traditions of Memphis, and its chief god, Ptah. The text gives solid evidence that it was meant to be performed, with actors (usually thought to have been priests) taking the parts of the various deities and speaking the parts assigned to them, for example, 'Words spoken by Geb to Seth', and 'Words spoken by Geb to Horus'. The story was recited and explained to the ancient audience by a lector priest.

Another Egyptian text, the Stele of Ii-kher-nofret, an official of the Twelfth Dynasty, records his visit upstream, at the behest of King Senwosret III, to take part in the mystery rites of Osiris at Abydos. He mentions roles that he played in the drama ('I acted as the 'Son-Whom-He-Loves' for Osiris' – that is, he played the role of Horus, the son of Osiris). He refers to ritual actions that occurred during the play: 'I opposed those rebellious to the *neshmet*-barque, and I overthrew the enemies of Osiris.' And, finally, he makes reference to that point when the procession actually entered the temple of Osiris at Abydos: 'I accompanied the god into his house.'

Similar evidence comes from ancient Mesopotamia and from the ancient Semitic Ugaritic civilization on the coast of Syria. An Assyrian building inscription of Sennacherib (704–681 BC) states that the New Year festival house in the capital city of Assur had bronze door plates on the central entryway which depicted the battle between the god Assur (replacing the Babylonian god Marduk) and Tiamat, from the Babylonian epic of creation, *Enuma elish*. Sennacherib himself played the role of Assur in the ritual battle, which was part of the dramatic performance of the creation epic at the New Year.

The Sumerian cylinder inscriptions of King Gudea, of Lagash, mentioned above, form the most full account that we have from ancient Mesopotamia, and perhaps from any culture, of the entire process of cosmic temple building. One scholar, H. Sauren, believed that the Gudea texts formed the text of a seven-day 'mystery play', performed each year at the temple dedication feast. He assumed that groups of actors, perhaps extending beyond priestly circles, would have been carefully chosen for each year's enactment.

The centre point of ritual drama in the Mayan temple was the ballcourt. Ballcourts were an integral part of the architecture of the sacred plaza, as for example at Tikal, where the most important one was situated between Temple I and the Central Acropolis, and at Copan, where the ballcourt served visually to unify the plaza with the main acropolis. The ballcourt games were based on the myth of the Hero Twins, as recounted in the Popul Vuh. The sacred twins were born of the union of a daughter of a Lord of the Underworld with one of the sacrificed brother-pair, the two best human ballplayers. The divine twins represented heavenly bodies, and the ballgames, mostly played out between victorious and vanquished lords with the purpose of supplying blood sacrifice, represented the on-going battle between kings and the Lords of the Underworld. The cosmic battle was waged within the temple complex, on the ballcourt, where kings would actually don the garb of the Hero Twins and engage in combat with opponents dressed as various Lords of the Underworld. The victory of the king would be followed by the public spectacle of blood sacrifice, the blood that was 'the mortar of Maya dynastic life' (Linda Schele).

The Gudea inscriptions underline one of the most persistent themes in the ancient creation myths, which is that the purpose and meaning of creation is to be found in the culminating act: the creation of the temple itself. It was only with the founding of the temple that societies were thought to come into existence, since the temple cosmicized and legitimized the society and its kingship. The 'Heavenly Jerusalem' that is brought down to earth at the end of time, as recorded in the Revelation of John, and as is made clear in the Qumran Temple Scroll, is one vast temple. The city has become totally sanctified as a temple, which is the ultimate blessing that a city can experience. The texts also make it clear that if the temples ceased to exist, then the cosmic order on which the society was based, and which gave it its legitimacy, was withdrawn.

The theatrical staging of the creation myths and of the mysteries of the afterlife in ancient temples, with initiates playing various roles, was the central ritual process in a society that had been cosmicized by the creation of the temple. It reinforced the most important religious and psychological information needed for a satisfying life and hope for a glorious afterlife. Most importantly, as Mircea Eliade wrote: 'The profound reason for all these symbols is clear: the temple is the image of the sanctified world. The holiness of the temple sanctifies both the cosmos and cosmic time. Therefore, the temple represents the original state of the world: the pure world that was not worn out by time or sullied by an invasion of the profane.'

The House of Life

All of the great temple traditions have been literate. As soon as writing was invented, it was used to record sacred texts. Some scholars believe that writing was discovered in ancient Sumer and in Egypt under the impetus of ritual, and the concomitant need to record creation myths, rituals and other sacred histories. In any case, as soon as writing was invented in Sumer and Egypt, about the middle of the fourth millenium BC, libraries were built into the great temples to store many different types of texts, including business, diplomatic and sacred. The earliest libraries were temple libraries, and particularly in Egypt this institution is well documented in the form of the *pr 'nkh*, the 'House of Life', which combined, usually within the temple complex, a library, a scriptorium and a general college for the instruction in all the sacred sciences and the professions related to these sciences: medicine, art, architecture, sculpture, astronomy and mathematics.

It was in the Houses of Life that the religious books of ancient Egypt were both written and stored. They were the 'sacred [that is god's] books', 'god's words', 'divine writings'. These were classified as mysteries, and were not to be seen by the uninitiated. One text states, 'It [the House of Life] shall be very hidden and very large. It shall not be known, nor shall it be seen; but the sun shall look upon its mystery. The people who enter into it are the staff of Re and the scribes of the House of Life'.

Another text refers to 'the hymns of worship written by the staff of the House of Life and given to the head teacher of the singers, and the like shall be written in the books of the House of Life'. And, further, 'O all ye priests who penetrate into the words of god and are skilled in writings, ye who are enlightened in the House of Life and have discovered the ways (?) of the gods, who have penetrated into the archives of the Library and can interpret the mysteries of the Emanations of Re [namely, the sacred books], who are skilled in the work of the Ancestors and who open up (?) the heart of what is upon the wall, ye who carve the tombs and who interpret the mysteries . . .'

We know that Pharaoh Ramesses IV (1163–1156 BC) spent a considerable amount of time in the House of Life at Abydos researching the 'mysterious forms' of Osiris, and comparing them with all the other gods: 'I have not left unseen any of them all, in order to search out both great and small among the gods and goddesses, and I have found . . . the entire Ennead, and all thy forms are more mysterious than theirs.' It is probable that the entire afterlife literature that is so well known from the tombs, coffins and 'books' was composed in the Houses of Life. This included that most famous product of the Egyptian mind, the Book of the Dead.

This is not to say that there were not other, more traditional types of libraries attached to the temples, whose purpose was essentially only the storage of books related to the temple. These more traditional temple libraries are to be distinguished from the Houses of Life in that the latter were more far-reaching, comprehensive centres for research, composition, possibly instruction, and storage of books, all relating to the full range of the Egyptian sciences that were devoted to maintaining and perpetuating life. According on one scholar, the House of Life was actually the original temple. In any case, it was the resource from which the priesthoods drew their ritual information and instructions, their own training, the entire range of funerary literature and ritual, insofar as these were employed in the temple cult, and the ritual spells and prayers that were composed for devotees. Gardiner refers to 'magical spells intended for the use of the living' that were composed in the House of Life.

Perhaps no ancient temple fits better the pattern of creation texts used in dramatic ritual being stored in a library near the temple than the Temple of Baal, in the ancient Canaanite city of Ugarit (modern Ras Shamra), on the coast of Syria. The city of Ugarit (which flourished between about 1600 and 1200 BC), excavated by French archaeologists since 1939, has yielded some of the most spectacular and important remains of an ancient city and of its cultural heritage that we have.

The Temple of Baal was located on the acropolis of the ancient city, and nearby was a building identified by the excavator as a library or scribal rectory. It was in the ruins of this building that most of the epic and mythic texts in the Ugaritic language (closely related to Biblical Hebrew) were found. The so-called

Baal Epic, similar in theme to the Babylonian creation epic *Enuma elish*, depicts the divine council in heaven, the epic struggle between Baal (the son of the bearded god, El, the Creator of Creatures who lived at the Sources of the Two Waters) and the cosmic waters, personified by Yamm (sea). The highlight of the epic, as also in *Enuma elish*, is the building of the temples to the victorious god, in this case Baal, a temple of cedar, lapis lazuli, gold and silver, high in the fastness of Mount Zaphon, the cosmic mountain of the North.

Analogies with *Enuma elish* (which, as pointed out above, was certainly the text of temple dramas in the Assyrian capital of Assur), the nature of the Ugaritic epics themselves (like the Egyptian mystery plays, they are filled with dramatic dialogue between the divine actors), and our increasing understanding of the role of ritual dramas in ancient Near Eastern temples, plus the find spot of the texts themselves (in the house of a priest, near the Temple of Baal), all point toward the texts forming the basis of temple dramas celebrating the cosmic creation. Additional evidence points toward the Ugaritic epics being performed in the temple at the New Year, at which time there was a celebration of the cosmic creation, divine kingship and the cycles of nature.

Secrecy

The temple preserves and transmits the esoteric tradition, the mysteries. Access to the rituals by which these mysteries are transmitted in the temple is restricted, and the knowledge of them is supposed to be kept secret from the uninitiated. Even in modern society, where 'there are no more secrets', and accounts of the initiatic procedures of various temple communities are widely published, such publications still do not give the uninitiated genuine knowledge of the esoteric traditions of the community in question because a ritual is something that must be experienced in order for it to become alive. Reading about it is not enough. Further, in a living ritual tradition there are oral practices at work, 'secrets', which are known within the tradition by priestly functionaries, and which are passed on only in the ceremony itself. Anyone who has actually witnessed a temple initiation, such as I have described above, and has then read one of the books that purports to 'reveal' its innermost secrets will know the difference, and will know how much of the living ritual will have been left out of the book.

Another Egyptian text dealing with this subject puts us into the milieu of secrecy: a book of magic that was to be composed on the 20th day of the Nile flood: 'Thou shalt not divulge it. He who divulges it dies a sudden death and an immediate cutting-off. Thou shalt keep very far away from it; by it one lives and dies. It is only to be read by a scribe of the workshop (?) whose name is in the House of Life.' The logic here is very simple but also compelling: if a society possesses the temple ideology, then it will possess mysteries, namely the mysteries of creation, the afterlife, and cosmic matters in general. These mysteries will be dispensed to a select few in the temple through initiation ritual. Initiates will be commanded to keep their knowledge and experiences secret from outsiders.

The Egyptian religious literature is full of this, as for example Spell 114 of the Book of the Dead (in Faulkner's translation): 'I know it, for I have been initiated into it by the Sem priest, and I have never spoken nor made repetition to the gods . . . I have entered as a Power because of what I know, I have not spoken to men, I have not repeated what was said.' The concluding phrases of Spell 162 of the Book of the Dead refers to a secret book: 'This is a book of great secrecy – let no one see it for that would be an abomination. But the one who knows it and keeps it hidden shall continue to exist. The name of this book is "Mistress of the Hidden Temple"'.

The reasons for this secrecy, which strikes many in the Western world as bizarre, unnecessary, primitive, undemocratic or even childish, are that what is being done is sacred, holy, something revealed by the gods, not to be trampled upon by the uninitiated or by those who do not understand. There is a strict demarcation between sacred and profane space, although, as I indicated above, any space can be made sacred by an authorized spiritual master within a given tradition, or even by a direct revelation from divinity to an individual at a specific locale (Genesis 28:10–22 – Jacob's dream at Bethel). But once sacred precincts have been demarcated, through having become cosmicized, they can only be entered with great caution, with proper ritual preparations, and with the proper authority. Any other approach could result in disaster: 'And he slew some of the men of Bethshemesh, because they looked into the ark of the Lord.' (1 Samuel 6:19).

The aspect of secrecy is reflected in the architecture of the temple. Once the sacred temenos was established and oriented to the heavens according to the sacred geometry, it became off limits to profane activity and profane people. Ancient Norse sanctuaries, known as *ve*, were separated off from profane activity by a *vebond*, a string or rope, or by a fence, just as shrines in the Greek world were encircled by a red band, or as the Agora in Athens was surrounded and set off by a special kind of rope, the *perischoinion*. The very fact that temples were considered to be mountains, in touch with the heavenly spheres, meant that they were sited on artificial or natural hilltops, which gradually became higher and higher over hundreds of years of continued building activity; their very height, combined with ramparts, could make them inaccessible to the common people.

The most venerable symbol of the inaccessibility of the sacred temple precincts to profane activity, as well as the symbol of the difficulty of approach for the pilgrim, is the labyrinth. The tomb-temples of ancient Egypt, most famously the original Labyrinth, that of Ammenemhet III (Twelfth Dynasty), described by Pliny, were constructed in a maze-like fashion, analogous to the mandala. The construction, copied by Daedalus in building the Labyrinth of King Minos on Crete, was intended to create a difficult pathway into the centre for the initiate, and to protect the sacred mysteries from outsiders. Furthermore, since one of the central purposes of the sacred dramas was the reenactment of the death and resurrection of the god, the labyrinth played the role of stage, in which the sacred circular ritual dances were performed, and the god was protected from his [ritual] enemies. The earliest labyrinths that we know are the tortuous pathways into the depths of the Upper Paleolithic caves of France and Spain. Labyrinths were constructed into the floors of Gothic cathedrals, most famously at Chartres, where the mosaic maze was laid into the floor at the crossing of the nave with the chancel, on line with the main altar, symbolically protecting the Holy of Holies from direct access, or making that access difficult, as access to the centre must always be.

The numinous, the sacred, possess great power (called in the Biblical scriptures 'the wrath of God'), which, if desecrated, can unleash considerable destructive force. Obviously, people are not killed today for transgressing the strict rules of secrecy that are associated with temple ritual. Such strictures are now, and probably always were, as a general rule, metaphors for the loss of the spiritual power attained in the initiation by the individual who revealed the secrets. As Lohengrin says in the 'recital of the Grail' section in Wagner's opera, 'And its [the Grail's] power is sacred as long as it remains unknown to all.' In many cases, the secrets are culturally or ethnically based, and provide a stronghold of inner, communal strength against the inroads of outsiders whose influence would contribute to the destruction of social cohesion that is fostered by the rituals.

An inscription on one of the doors of the Temple of Edfu states: 'Do not reveal what you have seen in the mysteries of the temple.' The Edfu texts give us insight into the nature of restrictions on entry into the temple. The vast majority of Egyptians were forbidden entry. The south gate of the temenos of the Edfu Temple bore inscriptions which stated: 'It is the standing place of those who have and those who have not in order to pray for life from the Lord of Life . . . The place for hearing the petitions of all petitioners in order to judge Truth from Falsehood. It is the great place for championing the poor in order to rescue them from the strong . . . The place outside which offerings are made at all times consisting of all the produce of the servants.' In other words, this wall was the furthest extent of entryway into the temple precincts that the common people were allowed. And it was at this place that they offered up their petitions.

Similar restrictions have been common in many temple societies, although, in the case of Tibetan Buddhism, members of the general public, including non-Buddhists, are now invited to attend the most sacred, and, until recent years the most secret, temple (mandala) rituals. As His Holiness the Dalai Lama has said, the contents of the Tibetan rituals are now 'an open secret', and he wishes to ensure that correct and accurate information concerning these rituals be made available.

Since the ultimate role and meaning of temple ritual is spiritual, the only harm that can result from betraying the secrets is to the inner spiritual life of the initiate himself. Those who, in a modern, open society, observe a ritual with some degree of curiosity, without personal involvement or understanding, can hardly be harmed, and indeed will doubtless be blessed, by the spiritual power of what they witness. One of the greatest problems of secret rituals, now as in antiquity, is that some of the uninitiated spread grossly false rumours about the rituals, based on partial or distorted information. This is especially true of some of the Greek descriptions of Egyptian ritual (which most of the Greek writers were not able to witness first hand), and it is also true of those twentieth-century accounts of Tibetan ritual which emphasize the supposed sexual nature of the rituals.

The Temple as a Place of Burial

Most of the great temple building societies have believed in the power of the temple, that dynamo of life and of power that is built over the primordial mound of creation, to restore life after death. Thus temple precincts have often become centres for burial, and the rituals of creation include accounts of deities such as Osiris in ancient Egypt, who was restored from death to life. The earthly temple, a replica of a temple in heaven, gives human beings a glimpse of the eternal life that is lived in the heavens. Humans were separated from the gods at the time of creation, when they were expelled from the paradise that they shared with them. The temple, with its artificial, or in some cases natural, paradise, its tree and waters of life, is the centre point of existence on earth, the place where death can be overcome.

In Egypt, tombs were essentially temples in that they were cosmically oriented, involved the deceased in the underworld funerary ritual, and were places of resurrection. Tombs were places of primordial power, and in fact, the inner burial chamber of the Archaic Period mastaba royal tombs at Sakkara was covered with a mound of earth, reminiscent of the mound tombs of the same period from Abydos. This mound represented the primordial mound of creation, just like the inner sanctum of Egyptian temples. The tomb was the ultimate inner sanctum, where the mysteries of creation, death and resurrection culminated.

The tomb and temple could be united on the same spot, as in the funerary temple of Mentuhotpe (2061–2010 BC) at Deir el-Bahri. The king's tomb was built into the cliff at Deir el-Bahri, at the western end of the temple complex, and in front of the main shrine, where his funerary rituals could be performed.

The strongest connection that can be made in ancient Egypt between the temple and burial is based on the prehistoric cult shrine of Upper Egypt, the *Pr-wr*, or Great House, of the early capital of Hierankopolis. This earliest shrine was incorporated into the funerary architecture of the New Kingdom, where coffins were built in its shape, and in the Temple of Sethos I at Abydos, where the innermost chapels in honour of Osiris, Horus, Isis, Ptah, Amen-Re and Re-Harakhte were fashioned after the design of the primitive Upper Egyptian temple. Coffins also typically show the Egyptian sky goddess Nut, painted onto the inner ceiling, which adds the cosmic dimension to this 'sacred place'. The Egyptian inscriptions contain the phrase, 'Nut is the coffin.' Thus the tomb was assimilated to the temple, and both became places of resurrection.

The funerary rites of the ancient temples were associated with the underworld, where the power to overcome death, in the form of the sacred tree and waters, originated. The Eninnu Temple in ancient Lagash had, according to the inscriptions of Gudea, a chapel called 'the house in which one brings offerings for the dead', said to be 'something pure, purified by *Abzu*'.

Archaeological excavations in many parts of the world have noted the tendency for a sacred precinct to draw large numbers of burials to it. A classic example of this is a series of prehistoric temples at the site of Tepe Gawra, in northern Iraq. According to the excavator, Level XI in particular 'attracted considerable numbers of burials to its precincts'. This same phenomenon has also become clear through excavations around the Temple Mount in Jerusalem, where famous Hellenistic period royal burials are well known in the Valley of Kidron, flanking the Temple Mount on the east, and now, in more recent excavations, royal burial places of the Kings of Judah may have been discovered on the northern edge of the Temple Mount.

Likewise the temples at Angkor, in Cambodia, served as 'royal mausolea', which received the remains or ashes of deceased kings. The great French scholar, Paul Mus, relates the Buddhist stupa to the role of the temple as a place of burial: 'We have before us a sepulchre which is also in fact, a temple. It is a sanctuary tomb . . . The tomb becomes not so much a shelter for the dead, as a kind of new architectural body, substituted for the mortal remains of a deceased 'cosmic man' where his magic soul will live on and prolong his existence.'

The Omphalos stone at the Oracle at Delphi took the shape of the tumulus, the burial mound, which was analogous with the original mound of creation. It was actually thought to be the grave of the dismembered Dionysus. Through the Omphalos (the navel or centre of the earth) one gained access to the underworld and its mysteries. Life and death combine at this place and in this image, the one arising from the other. A characteristic ancient Greek libation basin, the *phiale*, was frequently made in the shape of a shallow, slightly curved saucer, with a hump in the centre. These were known as 'Omphalos basins'. The Omphalos rises out of the water that stands in the dish as an offering, just as in Egypt and ancient Israel the mound of creation was seen as arising up out of the primordial waters of creation. This is the 'living water', the water that gives life to the deceased for whom it is offered.

The role of the sacred mound in overcoming death is also tied in very closely with the ancestors, because, by definition, the dead, having been reunited with the sources of life in the underworld, are numinous, and begin at their death to exert these powers on behalf of the living. Throughout Scandinavia the sacred Althing, the place of law-giving, judgment and other royal acts, was located on a mountain, where, previously, the burials of ancestors had been sited. Examples have been preserved from pre-Christian times in Sweden where the king's throne, along with a monument honouring an ancestor, were located together at the top of a sacred mountain.

The site of Palenque in the Usumacinta River Basin of Mexico gives us an extraordinary example of the burial of a royal personage, centred deep within the heart of a pyramid temple. The Temple of the Inscriptions, dated to the Maya Classic Period (about the seventh century A D) seems to have been built to house the tomb of the exceptional individual buried there. The access to the tomb was constructed through a floor in the main temple, which was then blocked and hidden through elaborate masonry slabs and rubble. An interior stairway, roofed with corbel vaulting, led down to the burial vault, which was constructed six feet below ground level, as a cave deep within the earth. There, the excavator found a monolithic sarcophagus in the shape of a uterus. The skeleton (of Mayan king Pacal) was covered with jade. The sides of the sarcophagus were covered with bas-reliefs depicting ten of Pacal's ancestors. Each ancestor is shown rising through the cracked earth with a different species of fruit tree. The lid of the sarcophagus contained an elaborate carving of the Maya Tree of Life. The Tree of Life in Mayan mythology, the Ceiba tree, united the three cosmic regions, and provided food and drink at its roots. Here it rises out of the cave at the centre of the earth, the Mayan hell Xibalba, as the *axis mundi*. A celestial bird sat perched at its top, while a serpent wrapped itself around it at the Middleworld, or earthly level. As the trunk of the tree sank into the underworld, it was swallowed by the open maw of death. A stone tube connected the burial chamber, along the staircase, with the temple above, which provided access to the world of the living for the ancestors, who would communicate through the Vision Serpent, the deity that provided communication between the two worlds.

An image of the sun on its passage from East to West, in between the two realms of life and death, was carved at the top of the sarcophagus lid, since the descent of the sun into Xibalba would take the king with it, while its rising would assure the king victory over death. The Temple of the Inscriptions was constructed of nine distinct building levels, corresponding to the nine levels of the Mayan underworld.

Here we have in the Mesaomerican realm the same combination of temple centred influences that we have seen in several other cultures: 1) a temple on top of a pyramid that has been built with astronomical orientation suggesting the idea of bringing a heavenly model down to earth, creating the sacred mountain; 2) a burial deep beneath the pyramid, suggesting the idea that life comes originally out of the earth, and that death is overcome by returning the body to the depths of the temple, to the First Mother, where the primeval power of original creation is most powerful, and where the deceased will rise, like the sun, from the underworld. A divine Tree of Life rises up out of the depths of the cave that the temple shelters, and unites the three world regions. It was along the trunk of this tree that the deceased and the gods travelled from world level to level.

The connection between the temple, death, burial and the afterlife finds remarkable expression in the Book of Isaiah, Chapter 25, verses 6–8. The context here is the covenant feast which brings all people together after the New Year festival at the temple, where chaos has been overcome and the people can rejoice together ('On this mountain the Lord of Hosts will make for all peoples a feast'). Since the majority of people could not actually witness the ceremony in the temple ('On this mountain'), it was through the covenant making feast that concluded the temple ceremonies that they become partakers of the blessings of the temple renewal and of the cosmic renewal of society. In this case, however, the setting is the messianic meal which the Messiah will share with all people in the messianic temple at the end of time, when the ultimate enemy of cosmic unity, death, will have been overcome: 'He will swallow up death forever, the Lord God will wipe away tears from all faces . . . .' (25:8).

Within the Christian tradition, this passage finds its fulfilment in the Revelation of John, where the Messiah sits 'within his temple' (the heavenly temple that has descended onto the earth, like the messianic temple of the Qumran community, that has taken up the entire city of Jerusalem) and the throngs of people who have experienced tribulation 'he will guide . . . to springs of living water; and God will wipe away every tear from their eyes' (Revelation 7:15–17). Thus we come back full circle to the point where this essay began: the mountain as temple, with its life-giving waters bubbling up from sources deep within the primordial abyss, possessing the power to overcome death. The temple, perhaps the most powerful and all-encompassing expression of the sacred in human society, brings together in its architecture, its symbolism and its ritual the most central features of the religious life of humankind.

The idea of the sacred mountain persists even when religions change. This Christian calvary is built on the site of an Aztec temple at Cholula.

The idea of the temple as the house of God, a specific place in which the divine spirit resides, is common to all religions. Christianity received it from a long tradition going back into the remote past. In this detail from an altar by Crivelli, the Madonna della Rondine, late 15th century, St Jerome is shown holding a model of the Temple of Jerusalem from which the golden rays of divinity are radiating.

The Greeks placed the home of the gods on the highest mountain known to them, Mount Olympus, and many of their temples occupy high places overlooking cliffs. The ruined temple of Sunion stands starkly overlooking the ocean. Around it, as around the great temple of Athena, the Parthenon, processions and rituals marked the sacred festivals.

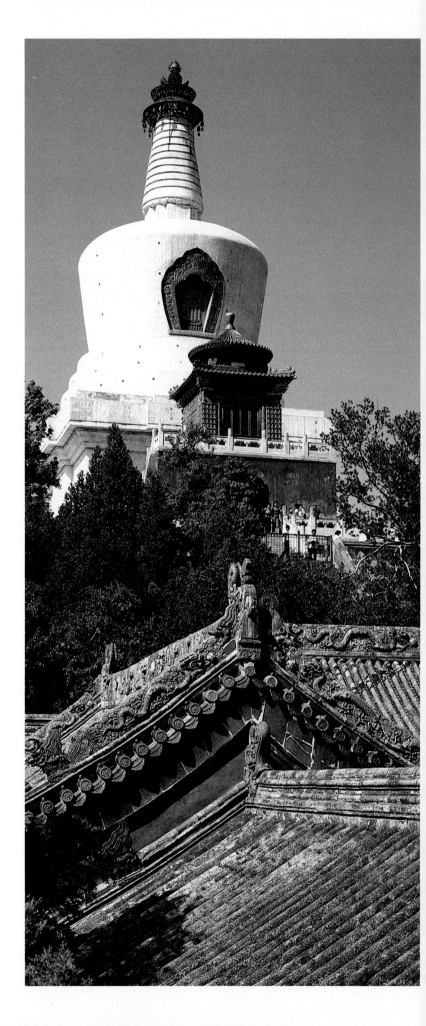

People in early societies identified mountain tops as the dwelling places of the gods. Later this belief gave way to the more sophisticated rituals of the great religions in which the form of the mountain was shown symbolically, from the ziggurats of Mexico to the pagodas of China. The Dagoba on Lake Beihai, in the Forbidden City of Beijing, is strikingly similar to the stupas surrounding the Sam-yē Monastery of Tibet in this Tibetan painting of the 18th or 19th century. Sam-yē, founded in the 8th century, is the oldest of Tibetan teaching monasteries, and the stupas of contrasting colours mark the four directions.

Following the image of the sacred mountain, early temples in many parts of the world are man-made mountains, so that structures as far apart as ancient Mesopotamia and Mexico are uncannily alike. The remains of the Babylonian ziggurat at Agar Quf has become so weathered that it could easily be mistaken for natural rock. The core is of baked brick and round its foot was a complex of smaller temples. The pyramids of Giza are the most perfectly geometrical of sacred structures, uniting the concepts of temple and burial-place.

Overleaf:
Borobudur, in Java, is the most complete example of the temple anywhere in the world, combining almost all features that occur in other religions. It is a sacred site, an object of pilgrimage, a symbolic mountain, an allegory of progress through rising terraces to divine revelation and an exposition in stone of a whole theological doctrine.

Mexican temples were invariably raised on steep-sided platforms and were approached by precipitous flights of steps: the Temple of the Inscriptions, Palenque. In Jewish and Christian iconography the same idea took the form of a ladder reaching from earth to heaven, most famously in Jacob's dream where he saw angels ascending and descending. Uniquely in architecture, the west front of Bath Abbey represents the Church itself as the ladder to salvation.

Water, which moves like a living being, has always been an image of the life of the spirit. Christ's own metaphor is represented in literal terms in a 9th century Gospel Book, when the fountain is itself like a miniature temple. In China real water surrounding sacred stones evokes tranquillity charged with divine force.

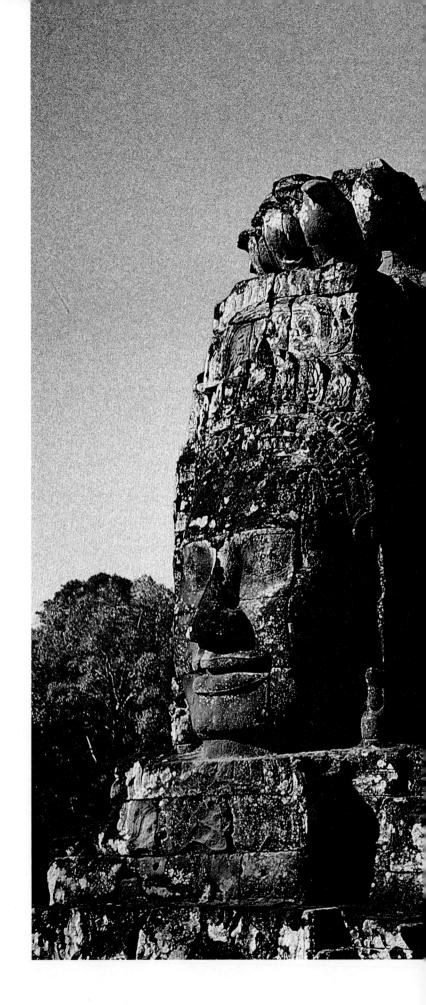

Not far from the main ruins of
Angkor Wat stands the comparable
monument of Angkor Thom, less
grandiose but better preserved.
These great heads on the central
section, the Bayon, represent both
the Buddha and the Khmer ruler
who built it, Jayavarman VII.

Common to all temples is the conviction that the divine person is literally present in them. Here the Hindu and the Christian artist – so different both in their apprehension of divinity (the goddess Durga in a manuscript painting attributed to Sajanu of the Kangra School at Mandi, c.1800–10, and the Virgin Mary in a Flemish diptych by Christian de Hondt, 1499) and in the architectural setting that they give her – still share a common vision.

49

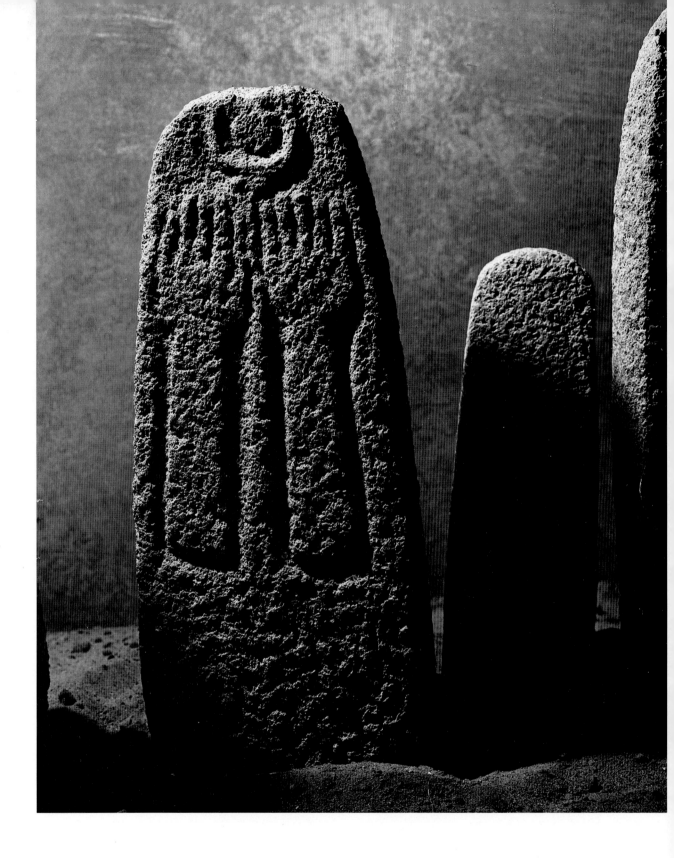

The most sacred place in the temple was hidden and difficult of access, and represented the dwelling place of the god himself. Mysterious when they were active cult-centres, they are inevitably even more mysterious today. The stele at Hazor, a Canaanite shrine near the Sea of Galilee, remains powerfully evocative of the worship of the moon-goddess, while amid the shattered stones of nearby

Byblos something of what the site
must have meant in ancient times
still lingers. The tall obelisks, once
capped with gold, stood in two
rows round a rectangular
enclosure.

Mount Kailas, sacred mountain of Tibet, is the object of one of the most devout and flourishing pilgrimages in the world. The holy mountain, source of the four rivers, stands for spiritual progress, raising the soul above worldly considerations as the body rises above the landscape. The 'New Jerusalem' is always thus 'builded upon a hill.' In a 16th century painting by Jean Lemaire de Belges of the 'Montagne de la Sagesse' wisdom is represented as a city on a steep hill, to which hard study is the arduous only path.

The Kaabah at Mecca – focus of Islamic devotion – is unique among temples. It was already a sacred place before the time of Mohammed, and according to one version of the legend had been built by Abraham and Isaac with supernatural assistance. Today every Moslem has a duty to go to it on pilgrimage once in his lifetime. This is a 17th century manuscript of Mirkhwad's *Rawdar al Safa*.

The laying-out of a temple involved exact measurement and alignment with the cardinal directions, and this process was often associated in mythology with God measuring out the Universe. In ancient Egypt it was symbolized by the Pharaoh stretching a cord, that is, surveying the site on which the temple was to be built (relief from the Temple at Edfu). Christian apocalyptic thought featured an angel with a measuring rod, seen here in one of the medieval Spanish illustrations to Beatus' Commentary showing the Heavenly Jerusalem (11th century).

58

The tree has been a universal symbol of the union of life at the human level with the underworld (the roots) and the heavens (the branches). Sacred trees are a feature of many religions. In Christianity the tree which bore the forbidden fruit in the Garden of Eden was sometimes identified with the tree of the Cross – Christ as the second Adam redeeming the sin of the first (wall-painting by Giovanni da Modena, c.1420). In Italy a wayside shrine is placed within a cage of pollarded branches. In India a goddess's shrine glows between two dark tree trunks.

The temple libraries were repositories of texts and images, some public, some secret, which together explained the mystery of existence. In the Egyptian Book of Caverns from the Tomb of Tausert, Thebes, the Sun as the centre of the universe is represented in three ways – as a child (inverted, moved by a pair of arms), as a ram-headed beetle and as a red disc. Worshippers stand on either side. The two triangles represent the black eclipse and blue stream through which the Sun passes. At the bottom a ram-headed bird spreads its vast wings. In Hindu mythology the universe is hatched from a cosmic egg (seen here in an 18th-century painting from Rajasthan), which has seven wrappings. At the bottom are the Tortoise, the Boar and Vishnu. From Vishnu's navel protrudes the lotus upon which Brahma sits. Above them come the seven levels of the underworld, then the earth with similar gradations and finally the peak of paradise where Krishna dwells.

Rising through many storeys, the oriental pagoda is another stylized version of a mountain, and is associated in the same way with circumambulation and processions.

The Porcelain Pagoda was drawn
by a European artist in the 17th
century; the Indian ceremony,
passing the temple of Sri Rangam,
dates from about 1800.

In the gory religion of the Aztecs, blood
was equated with the life-giving
streams that watered and fertilized the
land. Here (Codex Borbonicus, 16th
century) Cipactonal and Oxomoco are
portrayed as priests letting blood and
casting lots.

Water was among the first of God's
creations and retains its holiness,
literally or symbolically, in all the great
world religions. The figure in this
Egyptian fresco from a Twentieth
Dynasty tomb at Deir el-Medineh
shows the dead man, Pashedu, drinking
the waters of Amentit.

The temple's many forms

Throughout history, the urge to build temples has generated an instinctive impulse towards abstract geometry, though all its forms can be seen as in some sense originating in the primordial mound. *On this page*: the Ziggurat at Ur, as reconstructed by Leonard Woolley; the 8th-century Shore Temple at Mamallapuram, India; a section through the Mayan temple of Tikal, Guatemala; the Hōryūji pagoda, Japan; the temple at Philae, Egypt, drawn by David Roberts about 1838; and the Al Azhar Mosque, Cairo.

In the West, temples and churches have assumed a variety of forms, but all are recognizably religious. *On the left*: the Doric Theseion at Athens; the Gothic Cathedral at Cologne; and the 12th-century Norwegian stave church at Borgund. In 1922 the Expressionist designer Hermann Finsterlin made a series of models, a selection of which is shown here, reducing the forms of sacred buildings to their geometrical essentials. Egyptian pyramid, Islamic mosque, Christian church and Greek temple can all be generated from half a dozen simple elements.

The primordial mound

The first holy sites were probably
mountains. Today many of the most
outstanding shrines involve the upward
path and the deity who dwells in the
high places. Temples may be built on
the top of mounds, or artificial mounds
may be constructed for them, or they
may suggest the form of mounds in
their architecture. *On the right*: the 5th
or 6th century 'Royal Mounds' of
Uppsala, in Sweden, the burial cairns of
ancient Swedish kings; an Aztec throne
made in the form of a temple built on
top of a ziggurat; the ithyphallic image
of Osiris, shown reclining on the
primordial mound, on an Egyptian
papyrus.

Opposite page: two versions of the
Greek omphalos, the 'navel of the
world' at Delphi; a Buddhist stupa at
Sanchi, with its similar mound-like form
(*bottom left*); a black-figure Attic
libation phiale (6th century BC) with the
symbolic omphalos in the centre; and
(*bottom right*) a small votive stupa of
the 9th century from Nalanda, India.

The path inward

Temples use the image of the cave to express the numinous power of the inner journey and the still profundity of the holy of holies. In the Hindu temple of Phnom Kulen, in Cambodia, the sacred lingam stands in a man-made cavern (*right*). At Karli, near Bombay (*centre right* drawn by Thomas and William Daniell, c.1793), the temple is a real cave, and all the architecture and sculpture, including the elephants, the stupa at the end and the ceremonial umbrella over it, are all miraculously carved from the living rock. *Below*: the 'High Seat' in the inner sanctum of the temple of Horus at Edfu, Egypt. *Below right*: inside the Dome of the Rock, Jerusalem, which traditionally preserves the threshing floor above which King Solomon built his Temple. This was the spot from which Mohammed was taken up into Heaven, and which became the Holy of Holies.

Opposite: The deep recesses of caverns, with their darkness, mystery and symbolism of an inner journey, have been the shrines of gods for countless millennia (*centre left*: bison on the cave walls of Altamira, Spain). There are cave-temples in China (*top*: Mai-chi-shan, Northern Wei Dynasty), in Mexico (*centre right*: a Toltec initiate passing through the vortices of speech before returning to the home of the race to be born), and India (*bottom*: Indra's visit to the Buddha on a relief from Mathura, Uttar Pradesh).

The heavenly prototype

The purpose of the elaborate rituals that accompanied the choice of site, the laying out of the temple precinct and its consecration was to secure the god's approval, something which can be represented in art in a variety of symbolic ways. Mohammed (*left*) saw an angel bringing down the sacred precinct from Heaven, and by a similar convention St Augustine is shown inspired by a vision of the City of God as he writes his famous book.

Opposite
In a Tibetan wall-painting from Kantam a mandala, the concept of the temple in abstract, descends to a circle of priests from the heavenly sphere, borne by an angel. Jewish art could symbolize the divine presence only by a cloud, hovering over the tabernacle when it was erected in the wilderness – the earliest prototype of the Jerusalem Temple. The Renaissance sculptor Lorenzo Ghiberti, in his relief of the story of Cain and Abel, shows God appearing in bodily form above Abel's altar and rejecting that of Cain.

The site and the foundation

It was vitally important to choose a site pleasing to the gods, correctly aligned with the cardinal directions, and constructed with the appropriate ritual observances. In Egypt the pharaoh himself broke the soil with a hoe; this relief (*right*) comes from the temple of Horus at Edfu. The tomb of Senmut at Deir el Bahari has a ceiling (*far right*) carved with astronomical calculations which had to be mastered in laying out a sacred building. In Islam, every mosque has to be aligned so that the worshippers face Mecca, a point made schematically on this 16th century map of the Muslim World showing the Kaabah in the centre with lines radiating from it, upon which the various mosques around the Mediterranean are placed. Buddhist Japan had yet other criteria for the choice; in this 15th century scroll-painting (*opposite below*), Nichiren, the founder of a sect, searches the landscape for a temple site.

Sacred Geometry

The science of surveying probably arose through man's need to set out sacred buildings correctly. These feats of precise applied geometry are among the most astonishing achievements of the ancient world. The great temple-complexes of the Aztecs, such as Teotihuacan (*below*), involved huge ziggurats, ball-courts, processional paths and palaces all aligned on axes that could stretch for many miles. Equally impressive, on the other side of the world, was the building of Angkor Wat, a vast mandala in stone, a unique combination of mysticism and engineering (plan, *right*). The temple entrances all face west, so that the rising sun is aligned with the topmost

tower at the equinoxes and the
solstices. Many of the other towers
relate to astronomical correlations. On
a much smaller scale, a statuette of
Gudea, ruler of Sumerian Lagash in the
3rd millennium BC, holds in his lap the
plan revealed to him during the night
in a temple, that is as clear and
functional as any modern blue-print.

The divine presence

Unseen gods inhabit the temples that men build for them, and their presence can be shown only conventionally. In a 14th century Japanese painting from Kumano (*above*), the deities to whom the various shrines are dedicated appear above them in circular panels like portraits. *Right*: detail of a panoramic view of Wutai Shan, a region in Japan filled with temples, monasteries and sacred caves. Here the gods' presence is signalled by their appearance in a cloud that looks like smoke.

A Mesopotamian cylinder seal of the Akkad period shows five deities. The god of the abyss, Ea, strides across the sacred mountain at the New Year, while the Sun God Shamash rises from it. Ishtar, the equivalent of Venus, stands above Shamash. In Christianity, the use of images to portray divine beings has been controversial. Iconoclastic movements at various periods have insisted that God cannot be represented in bodily terms. More normally, images have been used to aid and embody the spiritual experiences of the worshippers. A 16th century icon explicitly places Jesus, the Virgin and saints in the chapels of a church.

0 ————————— 20m

Mandalas

A mandala is a geometrical pattern
embodying a spiritual truth. Brought to
its greatest pitch of sophistication by
Tibetan Buddhists, its essentials can
nevertheless be found in the religious
art of far distant times and places.
Mandalas can be drawn out on the
ground, and the plan of Borobudur
(*right*) – something which could never
be seen except with the mind's eye –
has all the characteristics of one.
Uniting the square and the circle, it can
work as the focus for meditation like
the classic Tibetan example, the 16th-
century Kalachakra mandala, illustrated
opposite (*lower right*). The back of a
Chinese bronze mirror of the Han
Dynasty, with its circle, square and
symbolic 'animals of the four quarters'
is also a recognizable form of mandala.
Other religions have used pattern,
symbolism and geometry in ways that
similarly represent mystical experience
in graphic form. Some are still
enigmatic, such as the engraved Norse
stone from Sanda, in Sweden, of about
500 AD. Others are luminously clear,
like the vault over the 6th century
chancel of San Vitale at Ravenna, Italy:
in the centre the Lamb of God,
supported by four angels; in the
corners peacocks, symbols of eternal
life.

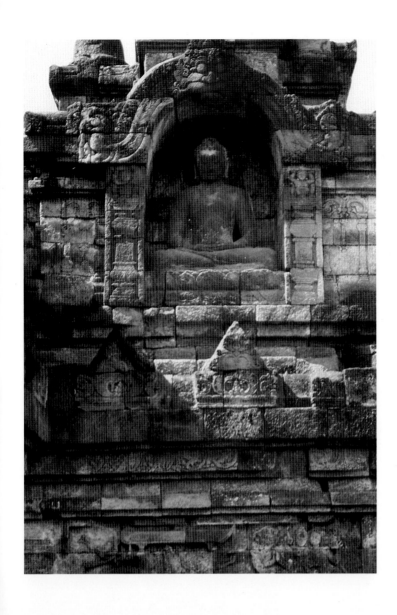

Borobudur

The great Buddhist shrine of Borobudur, in Java, is the most complex but also the most lucidly organized temple in the world. Its six lower levels are square, the four upper ones circular. Each level contains Buddha figures gazing out across the countryside in the cardinal directions. At the top are a series of stupas with square or diamond-shaped openings, originally each housing a figure of the Buddha. As pilgrims walked round each level they passed long sculptured friezes relating the lives of the Buddha on earth, so that there was both a circumambulatory and an upward movement, symbolizing the process of enlightenment through initiation.

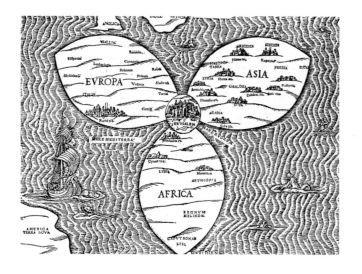

The Temple of the Lord

For the Jews there is only one Temple, that first built in Jerusalem by King Solomon, rebuilt by Herod the Great and destroyed by the Romans in 70 AD. Almost no trace of it remains, but throughout the Middle Ages Jerusalem was seen as the centre of the world. A schematic map of 1581 by Heinrich Bunting shows Europe, Asia and Africa like three petals springing from it. The first Temple was the resting place of the Ark of the Covenant (*centre left*, in a 6th century mosaic at Kwuzat Hefzibah, Israel). On the basis of written descriptions in the Bible, many extraordinary attempts have been made to reconstruct how it appeared, such as this by Bernard Lamy of 1720. Today part of its substructure is sacred to the Jews.

After the Muslims conquered Jerusalem they built the mosque known as the Dome of the Rock (below) over what was thought to have been the Holy of Holies of Solomon's Temple. It was a spot venerated by Islam as well as by Judaism and Christianity. When the Crusaders in turn became masters of Jerusalem, they transformed the mosque into a church and (with their limited knowledge of architectural history) took it to be the Temple itself. It appears prominently in such illustrated books as Hartmann Schedel's *Chronicle* of 1493, labelled 'Templum Salamonis', and in the backgrounds of several Renaissance paintings. It even influenced Jewish iconography of the Temple.

The way of the pilgrim

Pilgrimage is a journey to the divine source. It usually incorporates one or several of the features that we have found to be associated with temples: the ascent of a sacred mountain or the ritual of circumambulation. Islam has made the pilgrimage to Mecca (*top left*) one of the cornerstones of the faith. Every Muslim is bound, once in his lifetime, to make the journey and circumambulate the Kaabah according to the prescribed ritual. When he returns his house door is marked by a sign to show that he has accomplished the pilgrimage. In Buddhism, too, pilgrimage is an act of high merit. A pictorial map (*far left*) of the route to Mount Kailas shows eight of the monasteries along the way, with the holy mountain itself – white and conical – towards the left. The labyrinth is a symbolic pilgrimage and is found in many sacred contexts, from the Greek precinct of Epidauros (*left*) to the medieval cathedral of Chartres (*bottom left*). Something of the alert and strenuous atmosphere of the past can be recaptured in the Irish pilgrimage to Croagh Patrick, County Mayo, with its long line of men and women trudging uphill carrying staves.

The tree of Life

Trees are potent symbols of cosmic unity, their roots reaching into the underworld, their branches to heaven. The Judaic myth of the Tree of Knowledge and the Fall of Man is prefigured in Babylonian cylinder seals (*top left*) showing two figures seated by a sacred tree with a serpent behind the one on the left. The Buddha attained Enlightenment under a tree; a relief at Sanchi (*centre far left*) features the adoration of the throne and the tree. In Mexico, the Mixtec people were believed to have been born from a womb-tree (*bottom left*, from the Codex Vindbensis). But it was in Norse mythology that the tree attained its greatest prominence: the gigantic world-tree Yggdrassil (*centre left*) supported the cosmos, with sacred springs at its foot, a serpent at its roots and an eagle in its branches. This illustration is from a manuscript of the prose Edda of about 1680. A single column with a foliate capital can be a symbolic tree – as with that erected by Ashoka at Karli and the Qutab Minar at Delhi. Even in modern Christianity the association of trees with holiness lives on, as in this Thorncrown Chapel by E. Fay Jones, 1980, at Eureka Springs, Arkansas, USA.

90

The living water

From beneath the primordial mound sprang the rivers of paradise – recognition by early agricultural peoples of their dependence upon water for life. Sacred pools figure prominently in the religious rituals of the Aztecs and the Egyptians (*upper left*: the sacred lake at Karnak). At Angkor Wat, the imagery of water and of the churning of the Sea of Milk is part of the cosmic myth. Ancient Mesopotamia, born of the Tigris and the Euphrates, represented the primeval waters as stylized patterns on the façade of the 14-century BC temple of Karaindash, at Uruk. Biblical imagery of the four rivers flowing from paradise (*upper right*: a Byzantine manuscript of the 12th century *Homilies* of Jacob of Kokinobaphos), was given added mystical significance in apocalyptic vision (*right*), where the waters flowing from beneath the throne of God represent the salvation that flows from Christ's sacrifice (Flemish, c.1400).

The temple at work

Ritual is the technique or process through which the temple functions as a means of communication with the other world. Without the temple, it has been said, ritual is 'a map without territory'. Many of the rituals practised in temples were secret and have been irrecoverably lost. What took place in the ball-court of Copan, Honduras (*far left*)? We do not know with certainty. A sculptured alabaster vase from Uruk, c.3000 BC, seems to show a procession of priests bearing offerings to a goddess, while a painting from Khorsabad (*left*) represents King Sargon before a god. The Greek Eleusinian mysteries (*above*) are partially known from literary sources, though again some parts were kept secret. Some rituals took the form of dramatic performances which might prefigure the joys of paradise. Celestial beauties in the frieze of the Jain temple at Satnarjaya Hill, near Bombay, dance to the sounds of celestial male musicians. Egyptian ritual is also adequately documented on ancient papyri (*below*: Horemheb adores the falcon-headed Re, Shu and the lioness-headed Tefnut on a funerary papyrus of the Ptolemaic period). Such pictures gave later artists the clues to depict realistically the full panoply of an Egyptian rite amid the huge columns of Dendera (*bottom left*).

Life after death

Temples were the dwellings of powers who could overcome death, and were therefore favoured places in which to await resurrection to eternal life. Temples contained tombs and tombs were miniature temples. The so-called Tomb of Absalom (*above left*), just outside Jerusalem, is a Hellenistic structure carved out of the rock, traditionally identified as the burial place of David's son. Burial stones from Läbro, Sweden (*above*) and Mexico (*above right*) depict the soul's journey after death. Prominent on the Norse stone is the ship which carried the dead man's spirit to the other world. The Mayan sarcophagus lid records the burial deep inside the temple of Palenque of King Pacal. Far older, and most enigmatic of all, is the so-called 'Shaft of the Dead Man' in the prehistoric caves of Lascaux in France. It is possible that these caves were both temples and burial places. Here a very rare representation of a human being is placed next to a bison.

Further Reading

Benson, Elizabeth P., Editor. *Mesoamerican Sites and World-Views*. Washington D.C., 1981.

Bergquist, Birgitta. *The Archaic Greek Temenos: A Study of Structure and Function*. Lund, 1967.

Coedes, George. *Angkor, An Introduction*. Singapore, 1963.

Corbin Henry. *Temple and Contemplation*. London, 1986.

David, Rosalie. *A Guide to Religious Ritual at Abydos*. Warminster, 1981.

Davis, Richard H. *Ritual in an Oscillating Universe: Worshiping Siva in Medieval India*. Princeton, 1991.

De Vries, Jan. *Altgermanische Religionsgeschichte*. Second Edition. (Grundriss der Germanischen Philologie, 12). Two Volumes. Berlin, 1956–1957.

Eliade, Mircea. 'The Prestige of the Cosmogonic Myth.' *Diogenes* 23 (1958), pp. 1–13.

Ellis Davidson, H.R. *Myths and Symbols in Pagan Europe*. Syracuse, 1988.

Finnestad, Ragnhild Bjerre. *Image of the World and Symbol of the Creator: On the Cosmological and Iconographical Values of the Temple of Edfu*. (Studies in Oriental Religions, 10). Wiesbaden, 1985.

Gardiner, Alan H. 'The House of Life.' *Journal of Egyptian Archaeology*. 24 (1938), pp. 157–179.

Giedion, S. *The Beginnings of Architecture*. (Bollingen Series, XXXV, 6, II). Princeton, 1964.

— *The Beginnings of Art*. (Bollingen Series, XXXV, 6, I). New York, 1962.

Gomez, Luis O. and Hiram W. Woodward Jr., Editors. *Barabudur, History and Significance of a Buddhist Monument*. Berkeley, California, 1981.

Harrison, Jane. *Prolegomena to the Study of Greek Religion*. New York, 1959.

Kramrisch, Stella. *The Hindu Temple*. Two Volumes. Delhi, 1976.

Lawlor, Robert. *Sacred Geometry, Philosophy and Practice*. London and New York, 1982.

Lundquist, John M. 'The Legitimizing Role of the Temple in the Origin of the State.' *Society of Biblical Literature 1982 Seminar Papers*. Edited by Kent Harold Richards. Chico, California, 1982, pp. 271–296.

— 'What is a Temple? A Preliminary Typology.' *The Quest for the Kingdom of God: Studies in Honor of George E. Mendenhall*. Edited by H.B. Huffmon, F.A. Spina and A.R.W. Green. Winona Lake, Indiana, 1983, pp. 206–219.

— *Studies on the Temple in the Ancient Near East*. University of Michigan PhD Dissertation. Ann Arbor: University Microfilms International, 1983.

— 'The Common Temple Ideology of the Ancient Near East.' *The Temple in Antiquity*. Edited by Truman G. Madsen. Provo, Utah, 1984, pp. 53–76.

— 'Temple, Covenant and Law in the Ancient Near East and in the Hebrew Bible.' *Israel's Apostasy and Restoration: Essays in Honor of Roland K. Harrison*. Edited by Avraham Gileadi. Grand Rapids, Michigan, 1988, pp. 293–305.

— 'C.G. Jung and the Temple: Symbols of Wholeness.' *C.G. Jung and the Humanities: Toward a Hermeneutics of Culture*. Edited by Karin Barnaby and Pellegrino D'Acierno. Princeton, 1990, pp. 113–123.

Men, Hunbatz, and Charles Bensinger. *Mayan Vision Quest: Mystical Initiation in Mesoamerica*. San Francisco, 1991.

Mus, Paul. *Barabudur*. Two Volumes. New York, 1978.

Neumann, Erich. 'The Psychological Meaning of Ritual. *Quadrant* 9 (1976).

Neusner, Jacob. 'Map Without Territory: Mishnah's System of Sacrifice and Sanctuary.' *History of Religions* 19 (1979), pp. 103–127.

Nibley, Hugh. *The Message of the Joseph Smith Papyri, an Egyptian Endowment*. Salt Lake City, 1975.

— *Temple and Cosmos*. Edited by Don E. Norton. (The Collected Works of Hugh Nibley, 12). Salt Lake City, 1992.

Olschak, Blanche Christine, in collaboration with Geshe Thupten Wangyal. *Mystic Art of Ancient Tibet*. Boston, 1987.

Rappaport, Roy A. 'The Obvious Aspects of Ritual.' *Ecology, Meaning, and Religion*. Richmond, California, 1979, pp. 173–221.

Schele, Linda and David Freidel. *A Forest of Kings: The Untold Story of the Ancient Maya*. New York, 1990.

Soekmono, R. *Borobudur: Prayer in Stone*. London, 1990.

Stencel, Robert, Fred Gifford and Eleanor Moron. 'Astrology and Cosmology at Angkor Wat.' *Science*. 193 (July 23, 1976), pp. 281–287.

Tucci, Giuseppe. *The Theory and Practice of the Mandala, with special reference to the modern psychology of the subconscious*. Translated by Alan Houghton Brodrick. New York, 1970.

Von Simson, Otto. *The Gothic Cathedral*. Third Edition. (Bolingen Series, XLVII). Princeton, 1988.

Acknowledgments

The objects and illustrations reproduced in the text and plates are in the following collections:

Antwerp, Koninklijk Museum voor Schone Kunsten, Plaatsnijdersstraat 2, B-2000 49; **Athens**, National Archeological Museum 93 above right; **Berlin**, Staatliche Museen 90 below right; **Bologna**, S. Petronio 58; **Calcutta**, Indian Museum 70 below; **Carpentras**, Bibliothèque Inguimbertine (MS412) 52; **Copenhagen**, Det arnamagnaeanske Institut, University of Copenhagen. Photo Bent Mann Nielsen (AM 738) 88 centre; **Delphi**, Archaeological Museum 69 above right; Courtesy William K. **Ehrenfeld**. Painting illustrated in *Indian Miniatures. The Ehrenfeld Collection* (1985) 48; **Helsinki**, National Museum of Finland 78 below; **Istanbul**, Topkapi Sarayi Müzesi Kütüphanesi (Hazine 2154, 107) 72 above; **Jerusalem**, Israel Museum 86 below left; **Kwuzat Helfzibah**, Israel, Beth-alpha Synagogue 84 centre; **London**, Reproduced by Courtesy of the Trustees of The British Museum 34, 68 below, 79 above, 86 above, 88 above, 93 below right; Reproduced by courtesy of the Trustees, The National Gallery 33; By courtesy of the Board of Trustees of The Victoria and Albert Museum 62–3, 92 centre; **Mexico** D. F., Museo Nacional de Antropologia 5, 68 centre; **Newark**, Collection of The Newark Museum. Purchase 1920 Albert L. Shelton Collection. Photo John Bigelow Taylor, 1991, N.Y.C. 37; **Newcastle-upon-Tyne**, Gertrude Bell Collection, University of Newcastle-upon-Tyne 84 below right; **New Delhi**, National Museum of India 69 below right; **New York**, All rights preserved The Metropolitan Museum of Art, Helen H. Mertens Gift Fund 1973 (1973.11.3) 69 centre right; Oriental Division, The New York Public Library 20–21, 56, 60, 68 below, 74 above, 90 above, 92–3 below, 93 centre right; Spencer Collection, New York Public Library (MS No. 30) 72 below; **Paris**, Bibliothèque Nationale (MS Lat. 8850) 44, (MS Sup. P. 1567) 54, (MS lat. 8878) 57, (Codex Borbonicus) 65, (MS Ar.2278) 74 below, (MS Grec 1208) 91 above, (MS Néerl. 3) 91 below; Musée Guimet 81 below right; Louvre 77 centre left and below; **Recklinghausen**, Ikonenmuseum 79 below; **Stuttgart**, Staatsgalerie 67 right; **Vienna**, Österreichische Nationalbibliothek (Codex Vindobensis Mexicanus 1) 88 below; **Visby**, Gotlands Fornsal 81 left; **Washington** D.C., Freer Gallery of Art 75 below; Smithsonian Institution 78 above.

Sources of illustrations:

Photo: **Antikvarisk** Topografiska Arkivet, Stockholm (H. Faith-Ell) 95 left; *El Araby* Magazine 55; **Archive** for Research in Archetypal Symoblism 93 above right; Photo **Arthaud** 59, 70 above, 71 below left, 90 below left; Photo **Arthuad/M. Audrain** 71 below right; After F. **Baltzer**, *Die Architektur der Kultbauten Japan* (1907) 66 above right; H. **Baradère**, *Trois Expeditions du Capitaine Dupaix* (1834) 31; Photo Rologg **Beny** 35; Photo Museum of Fine Arts, **Boston** 38; J. F. **Champollion**, *Monuments de l'Egypte et de la Nubie* (1835–45) 60; E. **Chassinat**, *Le Temple d'Edfou*, vol. 12 (1934) 56, 74 above; Photo **Companía** Mexicana Aerofoto, S.A. 76; A. B. **Cook**, *Zeus*, vol. 11 (1925) 69 above left; Photo Roy C. **Craven** 66 centre left; T. and W. **Daniell**, *Antiquities of India*, 1799–1808 71 centre, 88 right, 89 left; *Déscription de l'Egypte* (1798) 20–21, 92–3 below; Photo Richard **Dormer** 51; Photo Dr Carolyn **Elliott** 87 top left; J. **Gailhabaud**, *L'Architecture du Vme au XVIIme Siècle* (1858) 86 below right; Photo Georg **Gerster**/John Hillelson Agency 40–1; **Hirmer** Fotoarchiv München 67 above left, 81 above right, 93 above left; Photo C. Greg **Hursley**/Hursley/Lark/Hursley 89 right; Photo Directorate General, Department of Antiquities, **Iraq** 39; Photo **Irish** Tourist Board 87 below; G. **Jequier**, *l'Architecture et la Décoration dans l'Ancienne Egypte* (1920) 90 above; Photo Russell **Johnson** 53; Photo A. F. **Kersting** 85 below; B. **Lamy**, *De Tabernaculo Foederis* (Paris, 1720) 84 below; Photo Richard **Lannoy** 50; Photo **Liu Lizhong** 73 above; G. **Loud** and C. B. Altman, *Khorsabad. The Citadel and Town* (1938) 93 centre right; Photo John **Lundquist** 36, 45, 69 below left, 82–3, 87 centre; Photo G. **Mazotti** 59 right; Photo Instituto Nacional de Antropologia e Historia, **Mexico** D.F., 68 centre; J. **Nieuhof**, *An Embassy . . . to China* (1669) 62; Photo Institut Géographique National, **Paris** 94 below left; T. **Patch** and F. Gregori, *Libro della Seconda e Terza Porta di bronzo della Chiesa di Giovanni Battista di Firenze*, (1774) 73 below right; Photo **Peabody** Museum, Harvard University 92 above; Photo Josephine **Powell** 71 above, 88 centre left; © **RMN** Paris 77 centre left and below; D. **Roberts**, *Egypt and Nubia*, 66 below; Photo: Robert D. **Rubik** NYC 20–21, 56, 60, 68 below, 74 above, 90 above, 92-3 below, 93 centre right; Photo Alberto **Ruz** 42; Photo Helga **Schmidt-Glassner** 67 centre left; Photo Wim **Swaan** 46–7; Photo Jean **Vertut** 64, 75 above; Photo A. **Villani** & Figli, Bologna 58; L. **Woolley**, *Ur Excavations. The Ziggurat and its Surroundings* (1939) 66 above left.